THE

TEST

OF THE

CENTURY

THE
TEST
OF THE
CENTURY

THE STORY BEHIND 1977's CENTENARY TEST

Foreword by Rick McCosker

Barry Nicholls

NEW
HOLLAND

To all the young dudes: Jacy, Ambrose, Harry and Ellie.
And
To the Southwood Family, where I spent many a day in the 1970s and beyond. Your generosity and encouragement of a young kid from up the road will never be forgotten.

FOREWORD

BY RICK MCCOSKER

Your memories are your life and life is so precious,
the friendships, the good times, the happiness, the sorrow,
your memories are your most cherished possessions,
safeguard them so you can pass them on — William
McInnes *The Laughing Clowns*

It is important for me to remember my roots—where I came from—and important to learn about those who have gone before me, whether they are my ancestors, or those who made the history of our great game. There were many history-makers over the first century of Test cricket between England and its 'colony', Australia. The greats and the good have all played their part in establishing the traditions that are the cherished possessions of those who love our game.

Anglo–Australian Test matches are the pinnacle, the dream of any budding Australian cricketer. Just to be there at the MCG during that week in March 1977 was, in itself, exciting, but more than that, an honour to represent our country, particularly in front of so many of the greats who had gone before us.

There are those who merely record history and there are those who write with passion—the latter's work is not just read with interest but with pleasure. These authors provoke memories that re-live the past in our minds.

Barry has captured, with authority and experience, the essence of this historical week in each chapter. In addition to capturing the importance and significance of this match he writes of the ensuing tumult that took hold of the game. Not just here in Australia, but in England, the West Indies and most major cricketing nations.

The idea that the cricketing Establishment was firstly to be approached for agreement and later to be challenged by an outsider was enormous. This was a major crossroad in the history of world cricket. However these events were preceded by a fantastic Test match that had tension, drama and quality cricket played by two evenly matched teams in front of magnificent and appreciative crowds.

There were many memorable moments during this match, but for me, I will not forget the singing of the crowd, the batting of Derek Randall and the courage, ability and endurance of Dennis Lillee as he bowled us to victory on that last exciting afternoon. And the realisation afterwards in the dressing room that the result was exactly the same as the initial encounter so long ago.

Many cricket books have been written, purchased and read by countless thousands of cricket enthusiasts. I suggest that this one will be of interest to anyone interested in sporting history and that it will most likely create a great deal of discussion, not only about the Centenary Test but about the ensuing changes to world cricket. Enjoy the read.

CONTENTS

INTRODUCTION

The Centenary Test means many things to many people. It was a celebration of Test cricket; a game played over five gruelling days that used every last physical and emotional resource of the players, played until the final hour of the final session. One hundred years of these encounters between the traditional rivals, Australia and England, was to be marked by one Test match in March 1977.

While traditionalists celebrated this grand occasion, for the progressives the match represented the junction between the old and the new. Amid the bonhomie of the two hundred plus visiting ex-players, Australia's cricketing elite was being signed by businessman Kerry Packer to play the first fully professional cricket competition in Australia, World Series Cricket. Secret meetings were being held in hotel rooms and bars where players signed up to a TV deal with Australian businessman Kerry Packer. It was, from the establishment point of view, as treacherous a move as possible. But this was all yet to be discovered.

Time magazine even featured a preview of the Test match on its cover under the title 'The Best of Enemies: Test of the Century'. England captain Tony Greig was pictured with bat in hand wearing an MCC sweater and Australian fast bowler Dennis Lillee was in the green and gold holding a cricket ball and looking sideways at his opponent. In describing the match, the magazine said:

> *The world of cricket has never known anything quite like it—not in 100 years, not ever. From Britain and South Africa, from the Philippines, Papua New Guinea and New Zealand, from Darwin, Perth and Adelaide, hordes of fans and commentators were descending on the staid but sports-mad Melbourne this week.*

The Centenary Test was a match out of season, played in autumn, normally a time when sporting minds have drifted away from cricketers in whites to footballers in club colours and overcast drizzling skies. By then the MCG had started to look more rain drenched than sun bleached; its green hues turning a shade darker as the days continued to shorten and shadows from the Great Southern stand, that resembles a Roman colosseum, lengthened.

The Centenary Test itself would forever be a reminder of the dangers of cricket. When Australian opening batsman Rick McCosker had his jaw broken by a Bob Willis bouncer and crumpled clutching his face we were reminded of the risks inherent in the game. There was also great beauty in the stroke play of the youngest player on the field, the fresh faced Test debutant David Hookes, who struck the English captain Tony Greig for five glorious fours in a row in what was as much a statement of Australia's intent as it was a tally of 20 runs from five balls.

The England side bowled Australia out for just 138 on the first day and the feats of Dennis Lillee, taking 6–26, helped dismiss England for just 95 the next afternoon. Later, a flattening out of the pitch enabled a close-to-record run chase on the final day. There was fearlessness in the century by Australian wicketkeeper Rod Marsh (the first ever by an Australian gloveman against England in a Test match) aided by McCosker's bravery in returning to the crease in the second innings, despite a broken jaw. But there was an English hero as well. Derek Randall's score of 174 against one of the best bowling attacks in the world marked him as a player able to rise to the biggest occasion in Test cricket history.

The contest was so even it ended with just half an hour to spare with the same result as 100 years before—a victory to Australia by 45 runs. You could not have designed a better finish to a game of cricket.

The Centenary Test was a lavish occasion with former players being flown to Australia from all over the world and it was celebrated with black tie dinners and cocktail parties. Australian cricket was on show for the world to see and it was a matter of damn the expense. The logistics of transporting so may past players to Melbourne and the organisation of various functions was carried out seamlessly. When the final crowd figures of more than 250,000 were tallied and compared to the meagre player pay of $400 a day, the figures provided more fodder for Greg Chappell and his militant band of players who were fed up with receiving such a pittance for being the best at their chosen art in the world.

For various reasons the Centenary Test's significance has grown in the past 40 years. The period marked the end of cricket as we knew it. The division point between the traditional ways of the past and the commercial direction of the future. Businessman Kerry Packer's shadow would loom large as his associates John Cornell and Austin Robertson signed the best players in the land——all in secrecy while the Australian Cricket Board were caught up in the celebrations of the Centenary Test. What followed, after a troubled tour of England in 1977, when news of Kerry Packer's World Series Cricket broke, was a war between cricket's establishment and the new breakaway group.

Packer would win this war handsomely and with it change the format in which cricket was played and marketed not only in Australia but also, later, around the world. Cricket would now be played under lights with one-day cricket one of the key fulcrums on which the game's attraction rested. Players became full-time professionals, leaving behind the days of having to cobble together an international career while keeping the home fires burning with casual employment.

The Centenary Test has gained greater poignancy with the premature death of the youngest player on the field, David Hookes. He represented the promise of youth and all that could be achieved if your dreams were large enough, but sadly Hookes was dead at the age of 48 after an altercation with a pub bouncer.

Other players too have passed, including the England captain Tony Greig at 66 after fighting lung cancer. There was also Bob Woolmer, whose death while coaching Pakistan in the West Indies during the 2007 World Cup remains a mystery. Woolmer's role in the match was limited to two starts as an opening batsman, a ruddy-faced Englishman under a hot Australian sun walking off in the twilight of that first frantic day

It lived up to the hype and was indeed the Test of the Century.

PROLOGUE: 1977 AND ALL THAT!

For many baby boomer cricket fans, it was our JFK moment; the 'where were you when?' moment. The first day of the Centenary Test at the Melbourne Cricket Ground in March of 1977. It was a Saturday and like many young cricketers across the country I was out playing for my school side on what was a warm and clear March morning in Adelaide. Pembroke were up against the might of Sacred Heart College, whose sporting prowess across all sports, especially cricket and footy, was renowned.

We were batting on the second day of our two-day match and missing one our openers whose dad had taken him across to Melbourne to watch the Centenary Test live. How envious we all were! As our under-14 team grew in confidence and started chasing down the home target it became increasingly clear that we might score more runs than Australia did in the first innings of the Centenary Test!

Transistor radios crackled as parents and team-mates brought out cordial drinks as the day heated up. The adults would talk in whispers of the score at the MCG, emphasising to us the importance of the information. It was a match that seemed to be captivating the nation. Even if you had wanted to you couldn't escape it in the media whether that be print, radio or television.

As news reached us of Australia's spectacular batting collapse, it seemed to defy all logic, a view that would come to represent many aspects of the Centenary Test itself as it was played out over the next five days. We knew that this was only the first day and Australia would fight back, as they always did. This match, that displayed the vulnerabilities of our heroes, and later their strengths, would become as Sir Donald Bradman said, 'One of the greatest Tests of all time.'

One of the great highlights of the Centenary Test was the gathering together of so many past players in one place. A simple search on You

Tube for the Centenary Test will find match highlights and interviews with many of the players.

Watching the video footage from 40 years ago is like seeing ghosts from the past.

There is Percy Fender, at the age of 84, being pushed in a wheelchair by his thirteen-year-old grandson Nicholas, who was brought along to describe the match to his near-blind grandfather. You can see the essence of the brash, young, aquiline-nosed Surrey captain who so boldly predicted in 1930 that Bradman didn't have the technique to do well in England. He later put the remarks down to an exuberance of youth.

Les Ames the scorer of 100 first-class centuries and England's wicketkeeper during that most brutal of series, the 1932–33, Bodyline series, is balding with thick, black-rimmed glasses, dimples and a beaming smile. He didn't like to talk about Bodyline any more. Watching the players mingle together it is as if the series never happened.

Old combatants, like England's former paceman Harold Larwood and the Australian batsman Hunter 'Stork' Hendry, sat next to each other on the flight from Sydney. 'What happened the last time you played each other?' ABC commentator Norman May asks. 'We'd better not say', says Hendry.

When asked how he was feeling, 72-year-old Larwood said he felt too shy and too old. England's dominating bowler of the 1932–33 Bodyline series hadn't been sure if he wanted to attend the celebrations.

> *I'm really glad I came now—I know I wouldn't have wanted to miss it. I didn't want to accept the invitation at first because I was a bit reticent, and I felt I was too old. But my wife kept at me and in the end I came and found out that everyone else had got old too.*

It is hard to imagine the fear Larwood caused the Australian batsmen all those years ago when he could bowl at 90 miles an hour and make the ball rise from the turf like a rattlesnake after its prey.

The fact sour memories had been forgotten was illustrated by the way

Larwood and former Australian batsman Jack Fingleton walked arm in arm around one of the cocktail parties. Forty-three years before, the Australian opener was dismissed by Larwood for a pair at the Fifth Test at the Adelaide Oval.

At one of the official functions Bradman was surrounded by Douglas Jardine's four fast bowlers—Larwood, Voce, Bowes, and Allen—causing Colin Cowdrey to remark:

> *The subject of Bodyline was never raised; the leg pulling*
> *was merciless, and I sensed in those few moments that some*
> *long standing tensions had been eased.*

It was a time of celebration and festivity. There was the Australian leg spinner from the 1920s and 30s, Clarrie Grimmett, who took his first wicket in 1925, looking like a grinning, bald eagle in a grey suit: 'I've got a picture at home of Frank Woolley, the first victim. I got 11–82 for the match.' He was right; there is a famous photo of Grimmett bowling the England left-hander in front of a packed hill that was part of a crowd of 40,830 at the SCG that day. Grimmett, light-footed and beautifully balanced, forever frozen with weight poised on his front foot having just delivered the ball. In his book, *Tricking the Batsman*, Grimmett stressed the need to always bowl the ball above the eye line to make it harder for a batsman to decipher the ball's length.

In the 1977 footage Grimmett walks with a stoop but you can still see that look of determination on his face. The ways his eyes dart from side to side when asked a question shows a mind that, in his playing days, had been alert to the opportunities a match might bring.

Then there's CE 'Nip' Pellew, who played in the first Test of the 1921 series, resembling an elderly landowner at the farm gate and with a sparkle in his deep-set blue eyes.

Gil Langley, who was the Australian keeper in the 1950s and once a federal politician, is round faced and smiling, wearing a tweed jacket as if he is about to give a class in philosophy.

A steely-eyed Godfrey Evans, when asked why he has mutton-chop sideburns, answers with a beaming smile, 'I have to wear these otherwise people might think I'm as young as I used to be.'

The 'youth' in the batch is Colin Cowdrey, who only two years before had faced the might of Dennis Lillee and Jeff Thomson. Cowdrey was on his seventh tour of Australia but this time didn't have to face the Australian duo. He still had the baby-faced appearance of his first tour in 1950 but looked noticeably more relaxed than he did on his previous visit.

The urbane, skivvy-wearing 1960s England captain Ted Dexter emerges, as does former England all-rounder Trevor Bailey, jet black-haired and full of smiles. Arthur Morris is shown seated with former England left-arm opening bowler Alec Bedser, who caused so many top order Australian batsmen problems with his ability to swing the ball in and seam it back out. When asked if he was Bedser's bunny, Morris politely points out that Bedser dismissed his opening batting partner more times than he did Morris.

Ray Lindwall, one of Don Bradman's Invincibles, was athletic looking with a sunburnt face and slicked back hair like a 1950s Hollywood movie star. And so the former players kept on coming some arriving more easily than others.

Reg Hayter, in the 1978 *Wisden Cricketers' Almanack*, wrote how former all-rounder Colin McCool was marooned in his Queensland home by floods and had to he hauled up from his front lawn by a helicopter and taken to the airport. Jack Rutherford's train broke down and he finished the journey to the airport by taxi. Dennis Compton left his passport at a Cardiff hotel and, but for an early start to the pre-flight champagne party at London airport which enabled a good friend to test the speed limits on the M4, would have missed the plane.

Christopher Forsyth, in *Pitched Battles,* described watching:

> *...old players stepping into the bars at the Melbourne Cricket Ground like instant television replays that caught them emerging fatter and greyer—but still recognisable—*

from the gilt framed photographs on the wood panelled walls of the Long Room.

There were hints as to how age had diminished their senses. Len Hutton was once an eagle-eyed batsman who in 1946 could spot the seam in Lindwall's hand at 24 metres. When he checked into his hotel he had to ask the porter to help him read the room number on the key tag.

Autograph hunters at the Hilton may have noticed Australia's top comic Paul Hogan and his production crew leaving the Hotel. The crew had found accommodation in the Hotel Victoria, a temperance establishment—a most unlikely venue for 'Hoges' known for his promotion of beer and cigarettes. The throng of former players was on its way.

THE FIRST TEST, 1877

Cricket is a game that rejoices in its history. As Frank Tyson wrote in his book *The Centenary Test*, 'Its dim origins are obscured by the shadows of the Middle Ages and the Sussex Weald, where shepherds first played the sport with their crics of staves as the bat.'

Its origins might be hard to determine but its official history is lengthy and full of folklore. International cricket dates back to a contest between the USA and Canada in 1844, but for the origin of what became known as Test cricket we must gaze upon the Richmond Police Paddock, now the Melbourne Cricket Ground when James Lillywhite's side representing England met David Gregory's Australian combination in March 1877.

By then, the concept of international cricket was not foreign to Australian fans. HH Stephenson's first English team came to Australia in 1861–62 and played against individual colonies. The sponsors, Felix Spiers and Christopher Pond, the proprietors of the Café de Paris in Melbourne, had originally intended to bring Charles Dickens out on a lecture tour but when he declined the offer they turned their attention to cricket instead and engaged 12 of England's leading professionals. George Parr's team followed in 1863–64 and then WG Grace's 1873–74 side.

James Lillywhite's 1876–77 tour of Australia was initiated after a proposal from Jos Pickersgill, a prominent caterer and former Melbourne Cricket Club committeeman, to bring GF Grace, the younger brother of WG Grace, out to Australia with a team lapsed. Lillywhite's venture involved an all-professional team helped by South Melbourne captain John Conway as an agent. Conway, who also helped choose the inter-colonial side, was a man of many talents. At various times he showed his abilities as a cricketer, footballer, journalist, agent, entrepreneur and, most importantly, had the respect of the players.

Tours in these days were a mix of long slow days travelling (steam boat, horse and cart and some rail), a packed playing schedule and official functions. Lillywhite's team of only 12 had been travelling and playing since they sailed from Southampton in September. Yet they sportingly agreed that after eight more games in New Zealand they would play a grand combination match, the day after their return in March.

This Grand Combination Match's uniqueness (the first ever Test match, as it came to be known), lay in its status as the first representative game played on even terms between an English touring side and an Australian side. Until then the visiting sides from the home of cricket in England were deemed so superior to what the Australians could muster—and generally were—that they played their side of 11 against teams of 15, 18 and sometimes 22.

History changed in 1877 when the Victorian and New South Wales sides had success against Lillywhite's tourists, thus increasing the call for a match on even terms. A game was quickly convened between New South Wales and the tourists, two days before the visitors left for New Zealand, which saw the home side having the worst of a drawn encounter.

Conway bypassed the Victorian and New South Wales Cricket Associations and approached the players directly to begin the process of organising the Grand Combination Match. The Victorian Cricket Association then coordinated a combined Victorian and New South Wales XI to play the Englishmen on their return from New Zealand. The side was to be made up of six players from New South Wales and five from Victoria. Victoria approached the NSW players directly (bypassing the New South Wales Cricket Association). This was a controversial move given that inter-colonial rivalry was very bitter in the days before Federation when you had to go through customs to pass from one state to another. It says a lot though about the sense of Victorian fair play that they selected Dave Gregory from New South Wales as the captain.

In what would be considered scandalous nowadays, the invited New South Wales player and the man considered the leading colonial bowler, Edwin Evans, declined to play for business reasons. Fred Spofforth was considered the next best bowler in the land and he refused to play because of the omission of Billy Murdoch, his preferred wicketkeeper.

New South Wales provided five players: Charles Bannerman, Nat Thomson, Tom Garrett, and the brothers Dave and Ned Gregory. Victoria's nominations were Jack Blackham, Bransby Cooper, Tom Horan, Tom Kendall and William 'Billy' Midwinter and Jack Hodges.

The local agricultural show in Warrnambool proved to be too much of a lure for Spofforth's replacement, Frank Allan, while left-arm fast medium bowler, Hodges, came in as a surprise replacement. One of the best players in the land, medium-pacer Harry Boyle, missed out on selection. There was speculation that Boyle's club, East Melbourne, had been in dispute with Lillywhite over ground bookings and therefore indicated its players would boycott matches against the Englishmen. Boyle was captain of the club so perhaps he felt an obligation to make himself unavailable despite his club team-mate Tom Horan being included.

Criticising absentees from 'a match that would be talked about for ten or twenty years' the morning *Argus* critic wrote:

> *Some players as they grow of fame need to be humoured, coaxed and petted like girls at the age when they don't know their own minds.*

The English XI was missing its wicketkeeper, Ted Pooley, who was left languishing behind bars in a New Zealand jail for his part in a betting scam. He had conned a patron, Ralph Donkin, into a bet in a Christchurch hotel saying he could forecast each man's score for the Canterbury 18. He would collect a pound for every one right and pay a shilling for every error. Pooley then wrote a zero beside each name and enough failed to score to ensure that Pooley managed a good return. Donkin felt he had been diddled and a fracas ensued. A court later acquitted Pooley but fined him for causing a disturbance. Feeling that the law had treated him harshly, sympathisers presented Pooley with a gold watch and 50 pounds before he set sail via America.

The Englishmen reached Melbourne only the day before the big match, no perkier for having to sleep on the deck on the voyage across the heaving Tasman Sea. Lillywhite's team's average age was 32 and a half while the colonials' was 25 and a quarter.

The England team consisted of the captain, James Lillywhite, Harry Jupp, Henry Charlwood, Andrew Greenwood, Thomas Armitage, George Ulyett, Alfred Shaw, Allen Hill, Tom Emmett John Selby and Jim Southerton.

Oddly, the match initially attracted little attention. When the crowd of 1500 turned up for the first day's play, described by the Melbourne *Argus* as a 'spendthrift waste of an autumn day', there were almost as many non-paying spectators sitting in the gum trees surrounding the ground. The crowd later grew to 4000 as the day progressed.

The start of the match was marked by barracking. Misled about the starting time, youths raucously demanded action. *The Australasian Weekly* found more pleasure in noting that 'when play began in sunshine the lawn was occupied by a numerous company of the youth and beauty of Melbourne.'

The smallish crowd was made up of heads of business and graduates from the well-to-do public schools, who were representative of spectators who had more leisure times to devote to sport than artisans and labourers.

Test cricket as we know it began on a sunlit March afternoon in 1877 at the elm-ringed Melbourne Cricket Ground. There were only four hours' play on that first day with the match beginning at 1pm and ending at 5pm.

The Australian captain, Dave Gregory, won the toss and elected to bat and the game began in clear, warm conditions ideally suited to cricket. Charles Bannerman opened the scoring with a single from Alfred Shaw's second delivery. His batting partner, Nat Thomson, was bowled for one in Allen Hill's second over. Shaw wanted to bowl with the wind and so Hill switched to the Punt Road end. He later bounced the ball into Tom Horan's glove which Hill took in the slips, dismissing the Victorian star for 12.

When Dave Gregory ran himself out for one he became the first captain to be run out in a Test.

Having scored a boundary and a single, all rounder Billy Midwinter stepped out and attempted to hit Jim Southerton over George Ulyett, fielding on the fence. But the Englishman held the chance, curving his back in the form of a bow and stretching up his hands. Had Midwinter hit the ball six inches higher it would have been written down as a five.

Bannerman counterattacked mainly with shots off the front foot, receiving strong support from, Bransby Cooper and Jack Blackham. Ned Gregory made the first duck in the annals of Test cricket when Andrew Greenwood caught him deep behind the left-hand bowler, James Lillywhite.

Alfred Shaw stood out for his accurate bowling while George Ulyett and Allen Hill proved brisk support and Southerton, at 49 the oldest England player to debut for England against Australia, bowled with guile.

England's lob bowler, Tom Armitage, was hit for ten runs in his first over and then attempted to pitch the ball high over the opener's head and land it on his stumps. When this failed, Armitage reverted to bowling grubbers, a technique not seen in Melbourne for 20 years.

At stumps Australia was 6–166 with opening batsman Charles Bannerman undefeated on 126, becoming the first century maker in Test cricket. Charles Bannerman was one of the three colonial players born in the British Isles. At 25, this agile migrant from Kent had seen some years in Sydney's professional clubs. Bannerman outlasted seven partners before retiring hurt on 165 ten minutes after the lunch break on the second day after being struck on the finger by a fast, lifting delivery from Ulyett. People who missed the opening day, fearing a one-sided game, denied themselves the sight of an innings which Lillywhite said Grace himself could not have bettered for resolution and brilliance.

Australia was eventually all out for 245 and Bannerman had scored 67 per cent of the total.

Australia's wicketkeeper, Jack Blackham, immediately caused a stir when he stood up to the opening bowlers. *The Age* reported that never before had a 'keeper stood over the stumps to the opening speedsters with gloved hands that were a blur to behold.' All this with thin pads and threadbare gloves, a far cry from the protection Rodney Marsh would wear 100 years later.

Australia's first delivery in Test cricket was bowled by Jack Hodges and would have resulted in a wicket had the umpire seen the English opener, Harry Jupp, accidentally knock the bails off. Not long after, Jupp played the ball on to his wicket with the ball failing to dislodge the bails. English opener John Selby fell at 23 for seven runs, prizing Hodges with the first Australian Test wicket. Jupp and Henry Charlwood added 56 and then a procession of wickets saw the visitors reach 4 for 109 at stumps. Word must have spread about the quality of the cricket with the third day attracting a crowd of 10,000. Billy Midwinter took 5–78 off 54 overs as England was bowled out for 196 with a first innings deficit of 49. When Australia batted again wickets fell at regular intervals. Australia was precariously placed at 9–84 at stumps with Alfred Shaw taking 5–38 off 34 four-ball overs.

A victory target for England of 153 seemed well within reach, or so thought the Australian public, with only 400 people present when play began on the fifth day (after a rest day on day four). Dave Gregory gave the new ball to Tom Kendall and Billy Midwinter, although it was Kendall, with 7–55 who won the day for Australia in front a 2000-strong crowd, with England scoring just 108 to give victory to the home side by 45 runs. It was a momentous win for the Australians.

It would take two months for the first account of the match to be published in England (in *The Times* on 14 May) where it was noted that:

> *The cricketers of 1877 prided themselves on the business*
> *of the beard. No fewer than 12 out of the 22 had beards of*
> *the 'birds nest' type and not one was clean shaven. Betting*
> *was carried out openly in the crowd and when play began*
> *the odds were in favour of England.*

Two weeks later James Lillywhite had the satisfaction of victory when his team won the Second Test in Melbourne by four wickets (played at the MCG from 31 March to 4 April.)

On 19 April a farewell dinner was arranged for the English side at the Globe Hotel in Adelaide, where Lillywhite gave Conway a locket for his help with the tour. When Lillywhite's side eventually steamed away on the *Bangalore* the waters were calm and the sky cloudless and good hearty cheers were heard from the shore wishing them godspeed.

Lillywhite's touring party reached Galle (in what is now Sri Lanka) on 8 May and then Brindisi in Italy. From Italy the players travelled overland across Europe before reaching London on 2 June. The tour in its entirety had taken ten months.

At the time these matches represented a giant leap for Australian cricket. The colony had somehow managed to defeat the mother country in a match played between sides of an equal number of players, a task previously considered impossible. Although some of the Australian players were originally from England, it didn't matter; the colony had triumphed and been cheered on by a sizable home crowd. Before Lillywhite's team had left Australia plans were in train for an Australian side to tour and play England on even terms in 1878. They didn't know it then but this was the beginning of the game that was later to be battled over five days and called Test cricket. The game would never be the same and international competition cricketing contests were here to stay.

CHAPTER 11

ANGLO–AUSTRALIAN TEST CRICKET

When we examine the 1977 Centenary Test and its significance, we need to consider how Anglo–Australian Tests were viewed at the time. As John Arlott wrote:

> *For long Australians maintained—and many still believe— that the term match applies only to a match between England and Australia. At various times South Africa and the West Indies have been stronger than either. Yet matches against those countries have never produced—reproduced would be the better word—the tension and high drama that invests every game between the two original old enemies.*

Arlott's comments summarise the attitudes of Australia and England cricket players and, indeed, fans. Until 1977, Australia and England Test cricket was seen as the premier of all cricketing contests. Other cricketing nations had experienced moments of dominance or provided series of similar stature but it was Ashes cricket that was generally seen as the best cricket at international level.

By 1977, though, a significant change in the balance of power was about to take place. Despite being defeated 5–1 by Ian Chappell's Australians, the West Indies dominated the England side of 1976, the year in which the South-African born England captain Tony Greig said he would make his

Caribbean opponents grovel. It's worth noting that this was at a time when South Africa was banned from playing Test cricket because of apartheid. Signs of change were in the air yet Anglo–Australian cricket was still seen as peerless.

The question needs to be asked: why did England and Australia hold sway in the manner they did?

This probably has something to do with the length of the contest and the nature of the relationship between the two countries. Dating back to 1877, Test cricket is one of the longest sporting rivalries in history. Another reason is the role that cricket has played in both societies. Since the codification of games in the mid-1800s, cricket became the dominant summer sporting pastime in each country.

The relative economic prosperity of both countries also enabled its countrymen to enjoy recreational opportunities, including the playing of sports such as cricket, providing a significant pool of quality players to draw upon.

One of the reasons that cricket at the highest level was seen largely as the domain of Australia and England must surely relate to the way the countries saw themselves as leading the way in a sport that somehow imparted traditional morals.

Cricket was the game that operated under strong ideals; a game we were told taught us about character. It had developed a strong foothold in English culture during the growth of public schools and the push for muscular Christianity emanating from Rugby College, and made immortal by the stories of Tom Brown's schooldays.

After all, the saying 'it's just not cricket' was used to describe something that was seen to be untoward or not playing by the rules. Cricket was a game drenched in tradition and mystique; evoking fantasies of glorious romance, it seemed to depict love of country, bravery and lofty purpose. A glorious manly game. Lord Byron remembering his boyhood at Harrow, sang of those days when 'our sport, our studies, and our souls were one:

Together we impell'd the flying ball:
Together waited in our tutor's hall
Together joined in cricket's manly toil

The 'idea of the gods' as James Barrie called it. Cricket was seen as a guide to life and providing a moral compass. The fourth Lord Harris, an England Test captain, described cricket as being, 'more free of anything sordid, anything dishonourable, than any game in the world.' Contests between Australia and England were supposedly full of such virtue.

The formation of the Ashes occurred after England's 1882 loss at The Oval helped spark a famous mock obituary that appeared in *The Sporting Times* on 2 September:

In affectionate remembrance of English cricket which died
at The Oval, 29 August 1882, deeply lamented by a large
circle of sorrowing friends and acquaintances. RIP. N.B.
The body will be cremated and the Ashes taken to Australia.

A mini ashes urn that was to be symbolically handed back and forth was created and a tradition was born. After a flurry of touring sides between each country (when players organised the tours and would make all the money), a more traditional pattern emerging in the 1890s when tours became less frequent with Australian teams visiting England every three years instead of two while English tours also occurred at three-yearly intervals.

The Anglo–Australian rivalry also reflected the way the relationship between the two countries was evolving. At the turn of the century Australia was moving away from regarding England as the mother country as it gradually began, at least symbolically, to cut the colonial apron strings.

The 1902 Australian team to tour England is seen as one of the strongest of all time. Led by Joe Darling it included star players such as Clem Hill, Victor Trumper, Reg Duff, Syd Gregory Monty Noble, Warwick Armstrong,

Ernie Jones, Hugh Trumble and wicketkeeper Jim Kelly. Australia won the series at Manchester with Trumper's 104 in 108 minutes before lunch on the first day the stand out performance. The series produced two of the most exciting finishes in history. Australia won by three runs at Old Trafford and England, after Gilbert Jessop scored 104 in 75 minutes, by one wicket at The Oval.

Australian cricket was never far from controversy during this period. As the first decade of the twentieth century neared an end the increasing friction between the Australian players and the newly formed Board of Control affected the morale of the team. When matters came to a head six of Australia's senior players (Clem Hill, Victor Trumper, Warwick Armstrong, Hanson Carter, Albert Cotter and Vernon Ransford) refused to agree to the terms of the tour. Australia had to send a second-strength side to England for the first-of-its-kind triangular tournament where Australia, although easily accounting for South Africa, was well beaten by England.

The long awaited return of Anglo–Australian Tests after the First World War occurred in 1920–21 with Johnny Douglas leading an MCC team to Australia in what amounted to one of the most one-sided losses in history. Australia's superiority was further illustrated on the tour of England in 1921 where the home side was demoralised by the hostile bowling of Jack Gregory and Ted McDonald.

Australia's dominance, which was led by Bert Collins in the mid-1920s, came to a sudden end in England in 1926 when each of the first four tests were drawn and England won the final one at The Oval, a win by 289 runs to regain the Ashes.

The cultural and social significance of playing cricket against England was highlighted in the 1930s.

In 1930 Don Bradman, a twenty-one-year-old from country New South Wales, on his first of four memorable visits, scored 974 runs in five tests at an average of 139.14 creating a new Ashes record and surpassing Wally Hammond's mammoth 905 set just eighteen months earlier in Australia. The highlight was his 334 at Leeds with 46 boundaries, a score that would go unsurpassed at Test level for almost 75 years. From 1930 on feats of such enormity would be referred to as 'Bradmanesque'. Bradman was small in stature at five foot seven, and slightly built at 10st 3lb, but had, in a short space of time, become Australia's mobilising force. Bradman's scoring was so unprecedented that 'BRADMAN FAILS' was a banner headline on Fleet Street one afternoon after he had made 80. After he was dismissed following his monumental 334 one London billboard simply said, 'HE'S OUT'.

England had a new master, a youth from Australia that they seemed to be able to do little about. The fact that England were being beaten in a game they invented, largely because of a young Australian batsman, made it seem all the worse. Bradman was a run-making machine who needed to be stopped. Some sort of response was required.

It wasn't long in coming. The 1932–33 Ashes series was full of aggro and ugliness. Author Keith Dunstan wrote that tension between the two sides rose so high that 'it was almost as if a state of war existed between Australia and England.' The idea of bodyline—a tactic meant to bruise a batsman into submission or cause them to fend off a catch—was born in a meeting between fast bowlers Harold Larwood and Bill Voce in the grillroom of the Piccadilly Hotel after the traditional Surrey versus Notts Bank Holiday fixture at the Oval in August of 1932.

The plan was carried out to perfection. England won 4–1 and Bradman's average was temporarily diminished to 56. Tensions between the two teams were at boiling point, Australia threatened to boycott the 1934 tour and even politicians were involved, warning that trade relations could suffer if the dispute wasn't resolved.

Bradman's final tour of a post-War ravaged England in 1948 was so one-sided that the Australian side became known as the Invincibles. They became the first Test match side to play an entire tour of England without losing a match after 112 days of play scheduled in 144 days. They won the test series 4–0 with one draw. Australia dominated because it had batsmen of the ilk of Bradman as well as Arthur Morris, Lindsay Hassett, Neil Harvey and Sid Barnes as well as the bowling strength of Ray Lindwall,

Keith Miller and Bill Johnston.

Bradman's popularity was such that the Australians were greeted with fanfare across the country and many records for match attendance were broken. Bradman finished the test series with the most famous duck ever made in test cricket, bowled by Eric Hollies at the Oval, but left England a winner with a test average of 99.94.

The tide turned in 1953 after a keenly fought series in which the first four Tests ended in draws. England won the Fifth Test at The Oval by eight wickets when Jim Laker and Tony Lock spun Australia out cheaply in the second innings. England's success continued in the next two series. In Australia in 1954–55 explosive fast bowler Frank Tyson burst on the scene, ably supported by Brian Statham, and Peter May and Colin Cowdrey guaranteed England would have enough runs to defend.

The name Richie Benaud is perhaps Australia's most famous cricketing name in postwar cricket. As Gideon Haigh wrote:

> *Few cricketers have matured so gradually yet ripened so fruitfully as Richie Benaud. With little to show for his first six years in Test cricket, he blossomed as a fully-fledged all-rounder in South Africa in 1957–58, then flowered as a charismatic captain at home against England in 1958–59. He repossessed the Ashes, which his teams then successfully defended twice.*

Benaud was part of early unsuccessful tours of England in 1953 and 1956, the latter of which saw England's Jim Laker produce the outstanding feat of 19 Australian wickets for 90—9–37 in the first innings and 10–53 in the second. No other bowler has taken more than 17 wickets in a first-class match, let alone a Test.

It was during the 1961 tour that Benaud came into his own in England. The tour was a personal triumph while Benaud's match winning bowling and clever leadership in the Fourth Test at Old Trafford proved decisive. With the series locked at one all England needed 256 runs to win and were expected to do so. Benaud, bowling his leg spinners around the wicket into the rough created by footmarks, took 6–70 to deliver an Australian win by 54 runs.

Australia won the series by drawing the final Test at The Oval and it confirmed a supremacy over England that would endure throughout the decade. Such was Benaud's ability to lead men, the then opposition player and later captain of England, Ray Illingworth, was full of praise for Benaud:

> *No captain of my time has impressed me more than Richie Benaud. Richie had the gift of making you feel you were a better player than you really were. He made his players believe he could win, even when the cause looked utterly hopeless. Nothing illustrated more clearly Richie's adroit handling of the men than his leadership in 1961. The Australian team should never have won the rubber with those players, but Richie instilled into them a belief in themselves—this attitude there is nothing we cannot achieve if we set our minds to it.*

Benaud's wise head was sought by Kerry Packer in the formation of World Series Cricket in 1977, conferring respectability on the breakaway professional circuit.

One of Benaud's team-mates on that successful 1961 tour of England, and later in World Series days as a cricket commentator, was a lanky big nosed opening batsman for Australia, Bill Lawry. The left-hander caught the eye with his elegant attacking strokes on the Ashes tour of 1961 but later pared his batting back, once even described by writer Ian Woolridge as 'the corpse with pads on'.

Lawry's courage was highlighted when he withstood fearsome attacks from Fred Trueman and Brian Statham in the infamous Ridge Test at Lord's in June 1961, and from Wes Hall and Charlie Griffith on an under-prepared Sydney surface in February 1969. Twice, too, he carried his bat through completed Test innings. The selectors treated him poorly, dumping him as leader and player for the final Test of the 1970–71 Ashes series. When World Series Cricket came along in 1977 Lawry joined Benaud as an enthusiastic co-commentator, belying his slow-style at the crease.

Ian Chappell took over the Australian captaincy when Bill Lawry was sacked. The culture of Australian cricket was changing. The Australian team's refusal to play an extra Test against South Africa in 1969–70 unless the players were paid more by the Australian Cricket Board was the first public show of defiance. The Australians' willingness to challenge authority was reflective of broader social change—it felt like people everywhere were protesting against the status quo.

Chappell's band of renegades played the same way they thought—no challenge was beyond them and they would win anyway they could, as long as it was within the rules. This was obvious when England toured Australia in 1974–75. With fast bowler Dennis Lillee recovering from potentially career-ending fractures in his back, England was confident that it would win the Ashes just as they had four years before. They did, after all, have a strong bowling line-up consisting of Bob Willis, Chris Old, Peter Lever, Derek Underwood and Tony Greig and didn't see the need to include John Snow who had helped skittle Australia four years earlier. They also had one of the leading run scorers in the world, opening batsman Dennis Amiss, as well as the capable batting of left-hander John Edrich and all-rounder Tony Greig as well as world-class wicketkeeper–batsman Alan Knott.

They hadn't figured on one-test failure Jeff Thomson being fully fit and a full-strength Lillee facing them when they arrived. England were destroyed by the dynamic pace duo of Lillee and Thomson as Australia took out the series 5–1, the only loss coming when Thomson was injured and Lillee left the field injured after just bowling a few overs (but still enough to dismiss Dennis Amiss for this third duck in a row).

Australia wasn't just aggressive on the field. In the face of growing financial pressure off the field they began to push for greater pay—not an enormous amount more. All they wanted was enough to ensure they could keep playing the game without jeopardising their security at home. Change would soon be on the horizon.

Cricket has always been the area where Australia has had the chance to meaningfully confront England on the sporting field. Rivalry between Australia and England exists in other sports, for example rugby, but not to the same degree. The dominance of Australian Rules football as a winter code meant there were no international rivals and Australia has traditionally never been strong enough as a soccer nation to establish a strong rivalry against England.

When looking at cricket and its effect on Australian nationalism, historian William Mandle argued it was, 'crucial to the building of national self-confidence. No other 19th century game carried the moral and even spiritual connections that cricket had come to bear.'

Cricket had also come to represent something important to the English psyche. Neville Cardus the eminent music critic and cricket authority wrote of the post-First World War years, when the war had greatly diminished the ranks of young Englishmen:

> *As disillusion increased and the nation's life contracted and the catchword 'safety first' became familiar and a sense of insecurity gathered, cricket itself lost confidence and character.*

To give some idea of how the players both past and present felt Norman May on ABC TV interviewed a number of former Australian and England players before the Centenary Test match and their views reflect just how high regard Ashes cricket was held in.

> *Peter Burge: England–Australia, as far as I am concerned they're the Test matches.*

> *Ian Meckiff: It's definitely a war that goes on out in the middle. It's been going on for one hundred years.*

Neil Harvey: An Australia–England series is the one. You seem to try that much harder against England than anyone else.

Sir Leonard Hutton: Neither side gives the other side very much.

All views illustrate how Ashes cricket was seen by the players as the real Test cricket. Other Test cricket mattered but it was your performance against the 'old enemy' that mattered the most. Hearing such comments gives some indication as to why the Centenary Test was seen to be so important. Although the Ashes were not being played there was great significance attached to this match.

One can understand the pressure the current players would have felt going into the match, given there were 218 former players watching the game. As Australia's opening batsman Rick McCosker said, 'It felt as if the whole of cricket history was watching on.'

Arlott again: 'These games have been fought on a high level, not merely of skill, but of psychological pressure which has searched out some players consistently successful on all other levels of the game, but found wanting in the fires of Anglo–Australian Tests.'

The feeling in the air was that the Centenary of Test cricket was going to bring about the greatest celebration of cricketing history that there had ever been.

At one of the functions hosted by the Victorian Cricket Association, Ray Steel, in his capacity as president, made it clear how important the Australia–England relationship was:

We are the original Test match enemies but when the battles are over we can get together and enjoy a drink, discuss the game and enjoy one another's company and this is what makes a Test match between Australia and England something very special for both countries. I think the remarkable thing to come out of this Centenary Test will be the remarkable friendships that are renewed. May this Test match be not only a historic one but also a memorable one played in the true traditions of English/ Australian Tests whatever that may mean.

The message couldn't be any clearer.

III
CHAPTER
III

CRICKET IN THE 1970S

Cricket, like society, was undergoing some rapid and profound change in the mid-1970s. For so long Australia's cricketers had been beholden to the wishes and whims of Australian cricket administrators. Australian cricketers had been part-time, having to try to hold down a full-time job while playing. Playing schedules were such that Australian players were often required to be available for six to nine months of the year although they were only paid in a piecemeal manner. Long, arduous tours, such as the one to the sub-continent of 1969–70 followed by a visit to South Africa, gave little consideration to the players' needs.

Cricket's change was being heralded by secret meetings in unlikely corridors initiated by an Australian businessman who had his heart set on gaining the exclusive broadcasting rights to Australian Test cricket for his TV stations.

In an interview with *Cricketer* magazine in February 1976 the cover story featured Australian captain Ian Chappell under the headline, 'Ian Chappell Scoop, Cricket's rebel answers all those questions you were afraid to ask.'

It had been a controversial time for Ian Chappell. He had recently stepped down from captaining the Australian side dubbed the 'Ugly Australians' and was accused of being the initiator of a greater degree of sledging in the game. His players wore long hair, casual clothes and had a confronting manner. The official uniform of the green and gold blazer and the baggy green cap ran in the face of the anti-establishment attitude.

Ian Chappell had a number of run-ins with officialdom for misconduct that varied from swearing at the umpires to dropping his pants mid-pitch. It was clear to Ian Chappell that cricket needed to move towards a more professional status.

> *The situation is improving, but that's no reason to stop it improving...Now I think the situation has been brought to a stage that should have been reached a few years ago. It hasn't been brought to 1976 proportions yet. But you've got to walk before you can run and we are moving in the right direction.*

Chappell's comments remind us that the players were not all out for revolution they simply wanted some more money for their services. The irony was that they didn't want much more money; just enough for Test cricketers to survive on from their cricket commitments.

When asked about Australian Test players becoming full-time professionals he responded:

> *I think it's feasible for Test players and in a lot of ways it would be advisable. It would probably make better players—they would be able to train specifically for cricket at the right times. At present most players have to work all day, then turn up to practice.*

Chappell was right. It was becoming increasingly difficult for both state and Test cricketers to be granted time off from their employers in order for them to fulfil their cricketing commitments. He had spoken to Sir Donald Bradman in his role as Chairman of the Australian Cricket Board to broach the topic of better pay but gotten nowhere. Bradman was against paying players their full market value and clearly had no idea of the players' frustrations.

Ian Chappell had a long history of railing against cricket's officialdom. In February 1976, *Cricketer* ran a diary recording the previous two years of Ian Chappell attracting headlines:

1974

August 4: Rumours fly that Chappell is about to be replaced by brother Greg as Australian captain. The reason; his language and colourful behaviour…

December 3: Chappell explodes over umpire Robin Bailhache's instruction of Australian fast bowers to keep the ball pitched up in fading light. 'It's pointless us being out there if we have to bowl the way the umpires tell us.'

1975

January 7: Chappell reveals he has been instrumental in asking the ACB for more money for Test players.

March 25: Chappell reveals he is fed up with cricket in South Australia, 'It's a joke the way cricketers in South Australia are prepared for first-class cricket.

June 17: Chappell defends a privately sponsored tour to South Africa, 'This will be a private tour and will in no way involve the Australian Cricket Board.

June 25: Chappell reveals the planned private tour is off.

September 1: Chappell heads a delegation of Australian players in London who meet with Australian Cricket Board officials and demand more money for playing Test cricket.

November 7: Chappell 'drops his trousers' in mid pitch

while batting to adjust his athletic support. The incident is captured by photographers and appears prominently on the front page of several Australian newspapers the next day.

November 11: It is revealed that Chappell will appear before the SACA over incidents during the SA–NSW match.

November 12: Chappell is warned by the SACA for misconduct and told if he infringes again he will be suspended.

December 8: Chappell is reported by the umpires for using abusive language in the South Australian–Victorian Shield game at the MCG.

December 12 Chappell is severely reprimanded by the Australian Cricket Board for using abusive language to umpires in the SA–Victoria match.

The reports read like a rap sheet of someone at odds with authority and desperate to change the situation for players. First-class and Test cricketers were poorly rewarded financially for representing their state and country. They had to request time off work and hope that generous employers would agree, and in some cases provide part of a wage during cricket commitments. Chappell had seen valuable first-class cricketers such as Ken Cunningham and Barry Causby retire from playing with South Australia because it was simply too hard to combine work and play.

Chappell was clearly frustrated with the way the game was being run and he garnered great respect from his players. As Mike Coward wrote in *The Chappell Years: Cricket in the 70s:*

> *To the most influential players of the day Chappell was a selfless visionary whose preparedness to confront the*

Establishment brought about fundamental changes in the game in Australia and beyond.

Chappell would later reflect on this period in Australian cricket

To me the big problem was that the ACB didn't sit down with the players and say, 'Look there's obviously a problem here. Can we get to the bottom of it and come to some sort of compromise?'

Former Australian captain Richie Benaud, who later became one of the game's most insightful and thoughtful commentators and writers, had been a mentor to Chappell and was well aware that modern day players had hardened their attitude to welfare and benefit issues since he retired from the game in February 1964.

The administration never cared. If you go back to the first book that Don Bradman wrote, there's a chapter on the 1936–37 (Ashes) series which drew more people and made more money than any other series...and he has a very telling end to the chapter where he indicates that it was very difficult for cricketers. They looked at all the money coming into the game but received small payments to keep the family, pay their own expenses and mortgages. It was something talked about over the years but something never, ever acted upon by any of the administrators.

As Chairman of the Australian Cricket Board until 1972, Bradman's attitude to money for the players was unchanging and a source of great frustration to Ian Chappell.

I think one of the most disappointing things about my relationship with Don Bradman was the fact that he didn't

have any sympathy for players of this period. I knew
Bradman had had a number of conflicts with the Australian
Cricket Board and one of them in particular, was over
finance. To me Bradman had as much to do as anybody
with the starting of World Series Cricket.

The match fee for the 1975–76 Worrell Trophy series was increased to $400, with $75 for incidentals. The players also took the lion's share of the $46,000 dollars in prize money distributed by Benson & Hedges, they received a bonus of $400 a Test. The takings of the Boxing Day Test match alone exceeded $310,000. The penny was dropping to players—they were missing out financially.

Ian Chappell resigned the Australian captaincy after the 1975 tour of England. His brother Greg a tall classically styled batsman, by then seen to be the best batsman in the world, was his replacement. His batting was cool and composed but never with a casual edge. He first played for South Australia as an 18-year-old before tightening his technique and toughening his mindset playing for Somerset, where in 1968 he made 1108 runs and took 26 wickets. His ability to embrace the big occasion was obvious when he scored a century in a televised John Player Sunday League game. He debuted for Australia at the age of 22 against England in the first ever test at the WACA. Coming in at 5–107 in reply to England's total of 397 he made 108 in four and a quarter hours joining in a partnership of 229 with Ian Redpath.

When the Rest of the World toured Australia after the scheduled visit by South Africa was cancelled, Greg Chappell again showed his class with scores of 115 not out at Sydney, an undefeated 197 at Melbourne and 85 at his then home ground of Adelaide. Success continued in England in the closely fought Ashes series of 1972 where he made two fine centuries, one at Lord's, and the other at The Oval. Chappell's century at the home of cricket showed his capacity for disciplined batting, his 131 occupied six-and-a-quarter hours.

An undefeated double century (247) and 133 followed against New

Zealand at Wellington in 1973–74, in a match where his brother Ian also scored centuries in each innings. At the beginning of that season he moved to Queensland as part of the state's quest to win its first ever Sheffield Shield. Against England in 1974–75 he managed 608 runs at 55. On the 1975 tour of England, at the Oval he and Ian Chappell became the first brothers to score centuries in the same test innings with their third-wicket partnership of 201 providing the foundation for an Australian win.

Greg Chappell hit 123 and 109 against the West Indies in his first test as captain of Australia at Brisbane's Gabba ground in 1975-76. Undaunted by the extra responsibility, he led Australia to a 5–1 victory in the series scoring 702 runs at 117. Although he was less a leader of men than his brother Ian, Greg became an astute tactician on the field.

His batting prowess was complemented by his brilliance in the slips. His seven catches at second slip in Perth in 1975 set a world record and Chappell's fourteen catches in the series was the second highest in a test series by a non-wicketkeeper. An elegant stroke player, while he leant gracefully into his shots he also drove powerfully on both sides of the wicket using a high grip. Bowling into Chappell's pads was trouble for bowlers with the ball invariably clipped to the mid-wicket boundary.

By the Centenary Test Greg Chappell had had enough of the relentless grind of international cricket along with the demands that captaining his country provided. He had been approached to join Kerry Packer's World Series Cricket and could quickly see the financial advantages in signing. He was ready to retire from Test Cricket and had achieved much of what was possible in the game. He now turned his attention to the Centenary Test having just returned from defeating New Zealand 1–0 in a two match series.

The cricketing environment of the mid-1970s was a vastly different beast to what it is now. There was only occasional one-day cricket in Australia. A domestic 40-over one-day competition, sponsored by the shaving company Gillette, that also involved New Zealand, was played on a knock-out basis. The Australian Cricket Board, while not revolutionary in its approach to change, was at least pro-active enough to organise the first ever one-day international when the Melbourne Test of the 1970–71 series was washed out. It had also shown enough flexibility to call off the South African tour of Australia in 1971–72 and replace it with a Rest of the World tour.

Gone were the halcyon days of the post–Second World War period when crowds used to flock to Shield matches in their tens of thousands. Small crowds attended the Sheffield Shield, the state domestic competition, although Test cricket was far less frequent meaning that Australian players often played for their state and sometimes also for their grade side. Life was different for spectators too. When you went to watch a game of cricket there was no entertainment away from the pitch, such as loud music or instant replays on big screens.

It was significant that the Centenary Test was to be played at the venue for the very first Test, the Melbourne Cricket Ground.

If you visited the ground in summer in the 1970s you would find *The Sun* and *The Australian* on sale at the ground for the early comers. If you sat in the notorious Bay 13 at the southern end of the ground, you would be certain at some stage of the afternoon to be sprayed with beer and be surrounded by a mass of fans chanting 'Lillee, Lillee' as Australia's premier fast bowler Dennis Lillee thundered in to bowl.

Many fans made their way to the ground via one of Melbourne's city trams, spilling out of the tram with a transistor radio glued to their ears, listening intently to all the previews on 3LO or ABC Radio.

This was the MCG that was built for the 1956 Melbourne Olympics and had all the hallmarks of a stadium twenty years old. The grandstand belonged to a different age. While some areas were undercover many spectators stood out on paved terraces. Seating was of the hard, wooden bench variety. The staple diet was a warm meat pie to match the warm beer available at the ground.

The move towards the corporatisation of sport was just beginning.

While cricket's administrators moved in slow, incremental steps with little forward thinking, the sands were shifting for cricket's sporting cousin, Australian Rules football. By 1977 there were the innovations of Sunday football, teams playing interstate and escalating transfer fees. The game was changing, although the fundamental structure of a twelve-club competition that operated under the same names and colours remained.

Cricket, though, had shifted little. Apart from the introduction of Tasmania in 1977 on a two-year trial basis, the premier domestic competition, the Sheffield Shield, was much the same. Test cricket was run the way it always had been by a largely volunteer group of administrators, overseeing players who were paid modest amounts.

There were, however, some similarities between cricket and the native Australian Rules football. There was a self-perpetuating paradox at play in both sports. Crowds were flocking in and sponsorship dollars had risen to unprecedented levels. However, in the Victorian Football League half of the 12 competing clubs were well on their way to bankruptcy. And Australia's Test cricketers' pay in no way reflected the size of the crowd at the ground or the TV audiences that they were bringing in.

The game had never been bigger or better or, indeed, looked better on television with the advent of colour TV.

IV

PACKER CIRCLES

By the time of the Centenary Test a number of factors were combining that allowed for the businessman Kerry Packer to sign the best players in the world for his own privately sponsored cricket competition. Cricket was booming during the 1970s when a young and marketable Australian team, full of personalities, easily accounted for England in 1974–75 and the West Indies in 1975–76. The uber-confidence of the Australians reflected the strong personalities of Ian and Greg Chappell, Dennis Lillee, Jeff Thomson and Rod Marsh. The open-buttoned, chest-out look initiated by Richie Benaud, combined with an on-field aggressiveness saw crowds flock to see this new brand of cricketing super hero. Other such as Max Walker and the seemingly laid back Doug Walters, whose ability to carve an opposition attack apart belied his public persona, added to the charm and appeal of the Australian side. Australia's fast bowlers were smiling assassins capable of cutting any international batting line up to threads. The Australians hunted as a pack, aggressive with bat and ball and able to take miraculous catches from the eagle-eyed slips cordon to the deadly accurate arm of Ross Edwards and the athletic Thomson patrolling the outfield.

Huge crowds were coming through the gates. Attendances at the 1974–75 Ashes were the largest since 1946–47.

The game's rising popularity was linked to better television coverage. This was highlighted during the 1970–71 series against England in Australia where, for the first time, a national telecast enabled viewers to watch the entire series. The television audience, by the later tests, was a million a day, about 50 times that of a live audience. Colour television during the 1974–75 series, and the introduction of slow motion replays, added to the entertainment.

The increasing popularity of one-day cricket was another important factor. One-day cricket had been introduced to English domestic cricket in 1963 where it helped boost the coffers of county clubs. The first one-day international, played in Melbourne in 1971 (when a Test between Australia and England had to be cancelled because of rain), attracted a crowd of 46,000. Just two months before, at the Gabba, a total crowd of 42,376 had attended the five days of the First Test of the series, clearly demonstrating the rising popularity and significance of one-day cricket.

The 1975 World Cup, held in England, further showed the potential of one-day cricket to attract a live and television audience. The final between Australia and the West Indies at Lord's drew a television rating of 21 at midnight, much higher than the average time-rating of 14 of Packer's Channel Nine. It was also a sellout at the home of cricket.

Forward thinking administrators might have considered the potential of the one-day game to attract a greater and more diverse audience to the sport. Cricket's financial value had also grown. However, the Australian Cricket Board was not forward thinking; the ruling body's attitude was rooted in an arcane, outdated, amateur view of the game.

Traditionally, cricketers were expected to have working lives and jobs away from the game. The honour of playing for Australia was deemed enough. Players were being offered what amounted to pocket money or what Ian Chappell called 'fish and chips money'. The result was that only a handful of players could stay in the game for more than a few years; they simply couldn't afford to play Test cricket.

While not completely amateur, the ACB operated with a full-time staff of no more than ten. The ACB had some money from TV deals, advertising and ticket receipts, which was funnelled back into financially propping up the Sheffield Shield and grassroots cricket. Most cricket administrators were volunteers, even at the state level. In 1977 the ACB sent Victorian

Cricket Association secretary Dave Richards to the US on a fact-finding tour to see how sports marketing really worked. But, in terms of cricket administration, the status quo remained.

The ACB, largely influenced by the conservative thinking of Don Bradman, believed cricketers should be honoured to play for Australia; the idea of financial reward for doing so was far from their minds. If the players complained, they were quickly reminded that they weren't professional. Alan Barnes, the then secretary of the Board's infamous remark that 'They are all invited to play and if they don't like the conditions there are 500,000 other cricketers in Australia who would love to take their place', very much reflected cricket administration's views. It must have been galling for the Australian test players to not be considered as professionals when English county players were. The Australians who played county cricket in the off-season could see just how poor their pay and conditions were and the fact that they had to tend to their injuries.

Dennis Lillee had complained to John Cornell, a Perth journalist and the manager of comedian Paul Hogan, that he was left with $30 a day for a Test after tax and deductions for expenses. This was for one the best bowlers in the world who was, for a time, also running a cleaning business.

The demands of Test cricket were certainly professional yet the pay was anything but. Had the Board scheduled more one-day cricket it would have provided an easy revenue stream to help increase player pay as well as keeping the game going at grassroots level.

But there were few one-day internationals scheduled. Between 1971 and 1977 Australia played fourteen one-day matches but only three were held in Australia. After the initial match in 1971 the ACB scheduled one against England during the 1974–75 series and another against the West Indies in 1975–76. These games attracted attendances of 19,000 and 14,000 respectively, representing fair crowds and a reasonable gate for limited overs matches.

1977 was a critical junction in the game's history. There was significant player disenchantment, although there had been a sharp increase in payments to players from the mid-1970s. The financial package failed to take account of the expanding cricket program, which required players to devote as much as eight-to-nine months of the year to the sport. This made it difficult for players to keep a job or look at changing careers. Players didn't have the certainty of an annual salary based on a contract and were paid in a piecemeal fashion after each test and tour. The players were also becoming increasingly aware that cricket authorities didn't consider player needs when scheduling tours in terms of travel arrangements, accommodation, food and rest days.

When Kerry Packer offered a fixed annual contract of $25,000 for a summer of cricket the leading players quickly signed. This was even though match fees were rising and no organisation existed to stage the World Series Cricket games, showing the strength of the players' discontent and how badly the ACB had misjudged their mood.

Kerry Packer and cricket will forever be associated because of World Series Cricket but in 1977, before the Centenary Test, his name was known mainly by those in the business world. The Packer family story, so the legend goes, was born one day in 1908 when a young Tasmanian, Robert Clyde Packer, found a dollar bill on the ground at a racetrack and backed a rank outsider that came romping home. He used the winnings to pay his fare to the mainland and fulfil his dream of becoming a journalist. By the time he died on a cruise ship he had amassed a media empire and played a bit part in the 1932–33 Bodyline series by insisting the cricketing journalist, Don Bradman, honour his newspaper contract, almost causing him to miss playing the series. Robert Packer's son, Frank Packer, expanded the empire to include some commercial TV stations and when he died he passed the baton to his son Kerry, a keen television watcher, cricket fan and aggressive businessman.

In 1977 Kerry Packer was not the major figure that we know him as today. He was in his late thirties, married with two small children and a bit of an unknown quantity.

Packer had founded *Cleo* and revived *The Women's Weekly* and had moved to Consolidated Press' broadcasting arm, Publishing and Broadcasting Ltd and launched into primetime drama with *The Sullivans* and *The Young*

Doctors. Despite these moves he was still seen as someone making his mark rather than dominating an industry as he later would.

In the mid-1970s Kerry Packer recognised that television sport was attractive, high rating and a cheap option. By 1977 he needed cheap Australian television content for his broadcasting networks, as the government had introduced a quota system requiring a certain amount of Australian-made content. For Packer, cricket fit the bill with its numerous breaks for commercials with the change of ends at the conclusion of each over. An added advantage of cricket was that it was a strong way of attracting advertising revenue during the quieter Christmas–New Year period. Packer's interest in the game intensified when he was told that the ABC obtained a rating of 21 at midnight for the 1975 World Cup final, live from Lord's.

Since the start of television in Australia the ACB had sold rights to both the ABC and commercial broadcasters. The ABC was always there and it covered all forms of cricket, including the Sheffield Shield. Commercial broadcasters occasionally took up the offer to broadcast cricket, for example GTV-9 broadcast the final Test of the 1960–61 West Indies series and HSV-7 covered the 1975–76 Worrell Trophy series and it would also broadcast the Centenary Test. But, overall, the commercial stations wouldn't bid for the rights because they weren't exclusive and they knew that viewers would prefer the uninterrupted broadcast of the ABC.

In 1976 Channel Nine bid an enormous amount of $1.5 million after the Australian Cricket Board invited bids for the next three years' TV rights to Australian home Test matches. Packer's request for exclusive rights was unprecedented. No commercial broadcaster had ever expressed dissatisfaction with a non-exclusive deal or presented itself as an alternative to the ABC. Packer at the time was asking of a lot for his group of television stations (he owned two TV stations TCN-9 in Sydney and GTV-9 in Melbourne which networked through other independently owned channel Nines, but a good deal of regional Australia was beyond its reach).

The ABC's bid was an eighth of what Packer's had been yet it won out for no obvious reason other than loyalty to the national broadcaster that had held the rights for twenty years. The ACB also persuaded the English Test and County Cricket Board (TCCB) to grant the Australian TV rights for the forthcoming Ashes series in England to the ABC despite there again being a higher offer on the table from Channel Nine.

In 1977 cricket in Australia was hugely popular and hadn't been so popular since Bradman. It was for this reason that Packer wanted the broadcast rights to cover it. Cricket was big for a variety of reasons. One was that the Australian side was a once in a generation star clustered line-up of players like the Chappells, Lillee, Marsh and Walters. Players, who not only played spectacular cricket but also had a touch of arrogance that only endeared them to the Australian public. They were proud Australians who were aggressive, larger-than-life characters.

Cricket in Australia was strong because of the way it was set up. There was a robust pyramid structure of junior, club and interstate cricket, which helped nurture and prepare good cricketers to become great. It was a structure maintained by thousands of devoted administrators and coaches. Cricket was also well supported by the media, dominating the back pages of newspapers and honoured by a consistent and strong place on the ABC, giving it national coverage. Cricket's earnings were fed back into the game.

Packer saw the disparity between players' value and their pay and wanted to sign the best cricketers in the world to play in a private competition that would be televised on his two Channel Nine stations and their affiliates. He then sought to sign up players for a world cricket tournament running parallel to the official one. The great irony of the Centenary Test was that while Australian cricket officials were putting the final organisational details of the match together, Kerry Packer was busy signing some of Australia's best players.

When Dennis Lillee appointed the former Subiaco footballer Austin Robertson as his manager it was not to go to the Board to get a better deal but help him earn money from non-Board sources. Robertson was friends with John Cornell who worked with Paul Hogan, who had a new boss— Kerry Packer.

The move to sign Australia's best cricketers to play in a cricket competition for Kerry Packer had been on for some weeks via his associates John Cornell and Austin Robertson. What better chance for some more signings than the Centenary Test where so many had gathered either to play or watch this grand occasion?

Packer's foot soldiers had a receptive audience. A number of prominent, disgruntled Test cricketers who had had enough of mediocre financial returns, were more than ready to break ranks. The final straw arrived when a number of players, most notably Ian Chappell, heard the gate takings from the Melbourne Test of 1974–75 of more than quarter of a million dollars ($251,771) from the well-attended five-day Test including a crowd of 77,000 on the first day. The players were getting only $200 a match. You didn't have to be a genius to work out that the players weren't getting the lion's share of the profit.

Players were also aware that sportsmen in other sports were considerably better off. Rod Marsh had a brother, Graham, who was a good golfer and who earned more than the Australian team put together. Australia's cricketers had no rival employer to offer more money. They had to rely on the goodwill of the Board, of which there appears to have been little. When Ian Chappell had presented his case to Don Bradman for more money for the players he was met with opposition.

One person who had been approached by the time of the Centenary Test but was yet to sign was the Australian captain Greg Chappell. The only person he had discussed it with was his wife Judy.

> I wasn't aware who had been spoken to and who had been signed. As Australian captain I'd felt a bit compromised, I was fine with the idea that if they wanted to go away and speak to everyone else they wanted to come back and to talk to me afterwards. I was concerned that if I signed early then they would run off the back of the Australian captain having signed rather than other issues and I didn't want that to happen.

Chappell would later sign a five-year contract starting at $50,000 and going up to $70,000 by the fifth year. It was an obvious choice for Chappell who at that stage thought he would bow out of cricket altogether by 1979.

It didn't matter much that Greg Chappell was yet to sign, as Ian Chappell had and that was enough for a lot of the players to get onboard. The fact that Ian Chappell was helping run the show was enough for them to sign; the money was a less significant consideration.

While Packer was willing to pay players a lot more than the ACB had— the money was comparable with a top professional in law or medicine—the players signed without even reading their contracts. In reality they knew little as to what was being proposed. They simply knew that they would be playing some games that would be on TV. No dates, venues team names and it was unknown if the matches would clash with Test and first-class dates. The players kept their contracts secret because they were urged to.

Packer, having been rebuffed by the ACB, was to experience the same from the ICC when he met with them on the 23 June 1977. What Packer wanted was rights to 'exclusive television contracts to cricket at the conclusion of the Australian Board's contract with the ABC in 1978–79'.

Packer was told that while the ACB would consider the principle of exclusive TV rights, it could only allow him the opportunity to bid for these rights on an equal basis with others.

Packer responded by scheduling each of his super Tests on the same dates as official Test cricket of the Australian summer and he took the ICC to court and won. Justice Slade said that the ICC 'had strained the bounds of loyalty' stating that the size of the profits of international cricket for years had carried the risk that a private promoter would appear and seek to make money by promoting cricket matches involving world-class cricketers.

Through what he would achieve with World Series Cricket, Packer would change the game forever and place himself in the spotlight of popular culture of the day. Packer provided the chance for Australian and world cricketers to play cricket as full-time professionals, and to take part in day–night cricket in coloured clothing as part of the whole lavish, corporatised television spectacular that modern cricket has become.

CHAPTER V

1977

By 1977 the changing social attitudes that developed in the 1960s were well established in Australia. More young people were living in de facto relationships and the anti-establishment fashion statements of long hair and a move away from wearing suits and hats were prevalent among young people. Gone were the days when Australian cricketers would wear their Australian blazer and a tie at formal functions. Former Australian opener and journalist, Jack Fingleton, would later write bemoaning the 'infernal tracksuit' that is often seen at Australian team practices.

Also gone was the practice of Australian Test cricketers receiving a carton of cigarettes each week they were on tour. By 1976 direct advertising of tobacco products was phased out by federal legislation however 'accidental or incidental' advertising was permitted which resulted in extended, prime-time exposure on television for cigarette brands. Television adverts promoting a particular brand of cigarettes were out but sponsorship signs within grounds that could be seen on a television broadcast of the match were still allowed. This meant that companies such as Benson & Hedges were keen to continue their sponsorship of cricket. Players often still smoked and were at times still employed by cigarette companies.

While we may view smoking through the modern unfashionable prism, in 1977 37 per cent of the population smoked (45 per cent of men and 29 per cent of women). Cigarette consumption per capita was at its highest since 1964 (3,200). In 1976 the ACB agreed to a sponsorship arrangement of $350,000 with Benson & Hedges and so smoking's link with cricket expanded.

Malcolm Fraser was Australia's Prime Minister and it was two years since the Dismissal, when the Liberal opposition blocked the supply of money after a series of economic bungles that culminated in Prime Minister Gough Whitlam being sacked by the man he appointed as, Governor General, Sir John Kerr. Back then future three-term Prime Minister John Howard was the country's Treasurer. The political landscape had been so turbulent during the preceding two years that Malcolm Fraser described the Australian public as 'almost punch drunk'. Cricket would soon mirror that turbulence.

In 1977 ABBA passed The Beatles in record sales and toured Australia from the end of February to mid-March with an entourage of more than one hundred, playing concerts in Sydney, Melbourne, Adelaide and Perth. ABBA mania was everywhere with 160,000 people attending their 16 concerts. Australians couldn't get enough of the blonde-haired blue-eyed Agnetha and the beautiful brunette with the fringe cut Frida, the lead singers of the band. Musical tastes, though, were changing rapidly, with Boz Scaggs (*Silk Degrees*), ELO (*A New World Record*), Fleetwood Mac (*Rumours*) and The Eagles (*Hotel California*) occupying the top four on the charts at the end of 1977.

The television show *Countdown*, hosted by Molly Meldrum, debuted in 1974 and was ruling the pop music airwaves. One of the first Australian TV shows to be entirely made in colour, *Countdown* was not only a champion of home-gown artists but also promoted international artists, helping give rise to the likes of ABBA, Madonna, John Mellencamp and Meatloaf.

In politics, the year marked the birth of the Australian Democrats, a merger of the Australia party and the New Liberal movement. Former Liberal Minister Don Chipp was the leader, vowing to 'keep the bastards honest'. It was also the year that would see the launch of the *Star Wars* franchise and 'a galaxy far, far away'. Special effects had never seemed so good and we were given a glimpse into a futuristic marketing world with *Star Wars* mini-figures and posters becoming ubiquitous. With its iconic theme a pop culture phenomenon was launched.

Fast food was becoming commonplace for Australian households with Pizza Hut, Kentucky Fried Chicken, Burger King and Hungry Jacks appearing first in cities and then regional streets. Instant tea and coffee were becoming more fashionable at home and in work places. In a look to the future of the finance world, the first automatic teller machine appeared in Fortitude Valley in Brisbane.

The Queen's visit to Australia as part of her Jubilee anniversary neatly tied in with the timing of the Centenary Test.

The Centenary Test was intended to be an event unlike any other in cricket's history. Timed to coincide with the dates of the first ever Test match in 1977, it would cross paths with the Moomba Festival, a large free community festival run by the city of Melbourne, featuring fireworks, water sports, live music and bands

The MCG had hosted some of cricket's biggest crowds. More than 77,000 had witnessed the first day of the 1974–75 Ashes series while more than 85,000 had watched the opening salvos of the 1975–76 Australia–West Indies Test. While large crowds were bringing spectators through the gates, the introduction of colour television meant television ratings were also high.

Despite the on-field professionalism of Australia's cricketers, Test cricketers were still largely amateur. Their training regimes were a far cry from the full-time professionals of today. Training consisted largely of a two-hour net session and fielding practice, not vastly different to the type experienced by grade and club cricketers.

The ACB itself was strictly part-time and unpaid, composed of honorary appointees elected by the associations among their first-grade club delegates. The ACB remained a non-profit entity distributing all the money it earned. They had no reserves, premises or employees. Australia's only paid full-time cricket administrators were the secretaries at each association. They oversaw an administrative structure that clearly worked.

The Channel Nine miniseries *Howzat! Kerry Packer's War* depicted Sir Donald Bradman as an unseen cricket administrator pulling the strings. But Bradman's influence on players and fellow administrators must have been strong—the greatest player ever to grace the game and revered around the world was the Chairman of the Board. He may not have benefitted from commercial arrangements during his time playing for Australia, but Bradman always pursued an alternative career away from cricket. He clearly saw a need for players to earn money away from cricket and demonstrated as much when playing, often working at his stock broking firm in Adelaide before walking down to Adelaide Oval to captain South Australia or Australia.

The Australian captain Greg Chappell says, 'cricket was in need of change', that it was travelling well but unless change occurred and there was greater consideration of the needs of players it would lose even more players. Chappell also wondered about the strength of the game outside of the traditional strong holds of Australia and England.

THE MCG

The one constant in the two matches of 1877 and 1977 was the ground. By 1977 the MCG had evolved from its basic form a hundred years before with just one grandstand into a top-level sport stadium capable of hosting a crowd of more than 100,000.

Visiting players were often intimidated by the Melbourne Cricket Ground and its vast cavernous size the first time they saw it. Colin Cowdrey never forgot the feeling as a 20-year-old of walking out to bat in front of 70,000 in 1955, 'like a Wembley crowd at a Cup Final'. He responded well, scoring a century. The sound that the MCG made when a good crowd was in and in full-voice was something you could get caught up in, the sound a bit like an aircraft taking off. The atmosphere as the sound bounced around the stadium was almost other worldly. The ground had a long and rich history of hosting sporting events. It had also hosted American troops in the Second World War and the evangelist Billy Graham when 130,000 turned up.

By the time of the Centenary Test it had been 123 years since the first match between the Melbourne Cricket Club and Geelong was played there on 25 November 1854.

The Jolimont site was previously a police paddock and first hosted an anti-colonial match against NSW in 1856. Conditions were crude although a small members' pavilion had been erected. By the time HH Stephenson's English team appeared in 1862 the MCG had improved significantly with a grandstand for 6,000 spectators and marquees to cater for the 45,000 who attended over the four days. By 1879 the club had erected the Northern stand, which the Englishman described as the finest in the world. This was known as 'the Reversible' because in winter the seating was reserved to face the football oval in the park to the north of the MCG. The reversible stand was burnt to the ground in 1884 and the club relocated to a different football venue at Olympic Park. A number of new stands at the MCG were built from the 1880s to 1914: the second Members' pavilion in 1881, a new northern stand for members and the general public in 1885, the Grey-Smith stand, mainly for the ladies, in 1906, an open Southern stand in 1882 and another open stand in 1900, the Harrison stand in 1908 and the Wardill stand in 1912. Most of these stands were built in red brick and in the Victorian or Edwardian style.

By 1977 its main grandstands consisted of the Great Southern (opened in 1936), the members pavilion (1928), flanked by the 1956 Olympic stand and the Ponsford stand (1967). It was a classic football stadium where, with a reasonable crowd, the noise made would reverberate around the ground. It was around this time that the infamous Bay 13 would lead the way chanting Dennis Lillee's name as he ran in to bowl. Bay 13 was seen as the epicentre of the crowd's poor behaviour, a place where prestige lay in counting the number of beers you had drunk that day. For the Centenary Test an army of 200 groundsmen were standing by to maintain the stadium at a cost of $5,500 a day.

CHAPTER VI

HOW THE CENTENARY TEST CAME TO BE

By the time of the match there had been 225 Tests between Australia and England. Australia had won 87, England 71 and 66 were drawn. There was one abandoned without result in 1970–71 due to rain.

The idea of a celebratory match was sparked by a conversation between committeeman Tom Trumble and Australian Test player and Melbourne Cricket Club vice-president Hans Ebeling. Trumble's father Hugh was, at the time, the leading Australian wicket taker against England while Ebeling had been a committeeman when the Club marked the Diamond Jubilee of Test cricket in 1937 and also helped plan the celebrations of the Club's centenary. Both had a keen sense of the game's heritage and worked on the logistics required to carry the match off.

The idea may have been Ebeling's but the man who had to deal with all the details was David Richards. He had joined the VCA as a 25-year-old assistant to Jack Ledward. Richards, an economics teacher and secretary at sub-district club Ringwood CC, had applied for the job on the spur of the moment. When Ledward contracted pneumonia and the immediate deputy Brian Cosgrove suffered a heart attack, Richards found responsibility thrust upon him. He became VCA secretary in 1973 and was authoritative enough to gain the respect of the press and young enough to be involved as the practice captain for the Victorian Shield side. Richards accepted the role of honorary secretary for the Centenary Test in September 1975. He worked for the next year collecting details of the 229 ex-players and officials in England and Australia, organising their accommodation at the Hilton hotel and the transport with Qantas and TAA. The Board had been reluctant to ask for more than twenty return flights for English guests but is was Richards who decided to ask for 93 and got them.

The marketing for the Centenary Test was like no other in Australian sport and it was no accident. David Richards had travelled overseas in May and June of 1976 with Tom Worrell, a former marketing manager at Nabisco. On a tour through the US and UK they took in Major League baseball and First Division soccer games, developing a range of ideas for the Centenary Test, including the logo, souvenir coins, stamps and medals.

As they celebrated Worrell's birthday at the New York Athletic Club, the birthday boy pronounced, after a couple of dry martinis, 'I think I'm going to go home and recommend we play cricket under lights in coloured clothing with a white ball.' Richards almost fell off his chair laughing. The joke was later not lost on Richards. Nor was the fact that for Richards the overseas jaunt was one in acknowledgement of the growing commercialisation of sports in the UK and US. He told *Australian Cricket* in December of 1976:

> *It was a tour undertaken to let me see how the major sports*
> *in those countries are coping with the financial strains of*
> *modern days and how they have advanced with the times.*

The organisation of the Centenary Test was an enormous logistical challenge, and all of this in the days before email and the internet. Invitations, travel details, accommodation, match details, commemorative stamps and memorabilia had to be arranged, all before a ball was bowled.

The Australian Cricket Board appointed the Victorian delegates Ray Steele, Bob Parish, and Len Maddocks to a subcommittee with David Richards as secretary. The subcommittee was charged with arranging all the details. Sir John Holland, representing the Victorian government's history advisory council and Hans Ebeling from the Melbourne Cricket Club were co-opted.

Qantas agreed to fly the former England players to Australia and TAA the Australians to Melbourne. The Melbourne Hilton accommodated the parties and Benson & Hedges sponsored the match.

The Centenary Test proved to be a party not just for the cricket fraternity but for the whole of the greatest sporting city in the world, Melbourne. There were constant reminders of the result of the first ever Test—an Australian victory by 45 runs—and a salute to Australia's first ever century maker, Charles Bannerman, and his 165 retired hurt, that guaranteed the home side a win. The numbers 45 and 165 briefly becoming as intertwined and enshrined in Australian cricket as the Don's average of 99.94. The first for the margin of the match Australia's way, the second for Bannerman's first inning's score. Images of Bannerman, until then a little-known opening batsmen, appeared in the newspapers and on television. Moustached and serious-looking, the Australian opener epitomised the new colonial spirit (although he was English born), coming to the fore in this most important of matches and scoring the first Test century. Bannerman only played three Test matches but was being reinvented as a hero. It was as if the retelling of the Bannerman story had breathed life into his own and his team-mates' bones.

The match's timing was odd but needed to coincide with the dates of the first encounter It was scheduled to take place after a long summer that had seen three home Tests against Pakistan and a three-Test tour of New Zealand. March was an unseasonal time of year for Test cricket in Australia. The Australian Cricket Board must have look longingly at the weather forecasts as the summer moved to autumn with the knowledge that many a district grand final had been diminished by rain. The weather Gods smiled and, apart from overcast skies on the first day, delivered beautiful clear, bright, sunny days. Although cricket authorities didn't know it at the time, the event that would swamp the Centenary Test was purely man-made and brewing like a storm cloud behind the scenes.

There was hope that the Centenary Test would deliver cricket's first ever crowd of 100,000 on the opening day and have an atmosphere more like a VFL grand final. Crowds of more than 110,000 were commonplace on the day of the VFL grand final. But this was cricket and it was different it involving six long hours sitting and watching. The record for a Test match was stuck at 90,800 a record set during the Fifth Test at the MCG in 1960 when Frank Worrell's West Indian team, with stars like Wes Hall and Garry Sobers, played the Australians as part of the classic series that involved the first ever Tied Test. If the Centenary Test could overtake it this would be a major coup and confirm the game's status in the Australian sporting landscape.

As the match approached so too did the growing sense of excitement as to what it might deliver. Special Australia Post stamps were designed. Jeweller and former Test player Ernie McCormick was asked to prepare sketches of a commemorative presentation piece for the players and the major cricketing bodies. To celebrate her Silver Jubilee, The Queen's visit to Melbourne coincided with the match.

Such was the significance of the Centenary Test that for the week of 14 March *Time* magazine dedicated its cover to the match with the heading 'The Best of Enemies: Test of the Century', with drawings of England's captain Tony Greig and Australia's fast bowler Dennis Lillee dressed in their team colours sizing each other up. Australian cricket sponsor Benson & Hedges incorporated cricket history into an advert with a two-page spread, cleverly contrasting photos of old-style bat and ball with the new. Within the spread was an image of Russell Drysdale's most famous painting, three country boys having an informal game of cricket against a building at Hill End. The town is deserted, there is unnatural light with the building's stark walls standing out. Across the three pages read the words, 'The golden era...In cricket as in life, some moments are...pure gold.'

One of Melbourne's hallmark trams was specially decorated for the occasion. Only a strike by scaffolding workers could put a dampener on the party. It meant the planned extension to the scoreboard, displaying full-colour pictures of past players, had to be put on the backburner.

The ABC and the 10 Network televised the match. Bob Simpson was part of the Channel Ten commentary team, as was Geoff Boycott. This was unusual for a commercial television network as there was a great risk in televising an event that the ABC also had broadcasting rights for, as viewers would often prefer to watch the commercial-free version.

To mark the significance of the occasion women were even admitted into the Pavilion when the Club had three open nights during the match. It also provides some insight into the attitudes towards women that some sporting clubs still had at the time.

Ten thousand visitors came from overseas and interstate creating the largest influx of tourists into Melbourne since the 1956 Olympic Games. It was the high point of establishment cricket and delivered a match befitting of a centenary celebration. Nothing left to chance, at least in the eyes of Australia's cricket authorities; or so they thought.

In the days leading up to the match Hans Ebeling was interviewed by ABC TV. Serious-looking, with a head full of white hair, Ebeling revealed how he was reminded of the need to mark the centenary:

> *The first Test was played at the Melbourne cricket ground in 1877 and it wasn't until I was just browsing through, looking for something and doing some research, that I saw the date again and all of a sudden realised it was only four years away and I thought that it was about time someone did something about it and the Melbourne Cricket Club took a leading part in the First Test in 1877 and I thought that we should take the lead in staging some celebration for the Centenary Test in March 1977.*

It was to be a time of great celebration. The Melbourne Cricket Club had three nights of an open house with members allowed to bring their wives. Invitations were also issued to country and junior bodies. There were no relaxations on dress though and the following edict was issued, 'Dress will be usual i.e. tie or cravat must be worn. Please don't embarrass yourself by coming in unsuitable attire.'

Four official functions were held—invite only: the Australian Cricket Board's official reception on Wednesday 9 March, the State Government Reception on Thursday 10 March, the ACB's dinner on 14 March and the Melbourne Cricket Club dinner on 16 March.

The Melbourne Cricket Club were making the most of the occasion with a range of club souvenirs including large and small steins with a print of the MCG 1977 on one side and the MCG 1877 on the reverse, ashtrays and carafes in stoneware with the same images, stoneware goblets, a wine set, an MCG tie, a strip photograph of the ground and members' area featuring twelve coloured pictures and a pictorial history of the ground with many coloured shots.

Every living Australian who played against England was invited to attend, as was every Englishman who had played a Test in Australia. The oldest invitee was Frank Woolley, at 89, who played his first Test in 1909. The oldest Australian was Jack Ryder, at 87, who played his first Test in 1920, although he was selected for the tour of South Africa in 1914 but the tour was cancelled because of the First World War.

The Australian newspaper also decided to use the Centenary Test as a marketing opportunity. There were limited edition print folios, six superb collectors' prints:

> *Never before has there been a collection like this in the noble sport of cricket. Not for another 100 years will there be an opportunity to commemorate an event as splendidly as with this historic collection of cricket memorabilia.*

The prints came with historical notes. If you were more inclined for the modern day scenes from the game you could also buy action photos by photographer Patrick Egar and a match summary from Richie Benaud.

As the match approached Greg Chappell wrote in *The 100th Summer* of his surprise at the excitement surrounding the match:

It is difficult to describe the atmosphere that pervaded Melbourne, immediately preceding and during the course of the Centenary Test to anyone who wasn't actually there to witness the event. From the moment I set foot in Melbourne...it was obvious the whole city was in the grip of cricket fever—something I hadn't observed in other parts of the country. Literally everybody was talking, reading and watching cricket highlights from the past and in the process having a whale of a time.

Umpire Max O'Connell was as excited as the players about the prospect of being involved in such a major cricketing event. At a cocktail party at the MCG two nights before the match O'Connell was talking to one of the Qantas jumbo jet pilots dressed in uniform. 'I'm taking the jumbo back to London and I've been given permission for a low fly around the MCG at twelve noon on the first day.' O'Connell thought he was joking but sure enough at drinks on the first day, 'It happened, the plane appeared the pilot flipped the wings and the plane disappeared up into the heavens.'

It was during the 1975–76 West Indies series that Australia's new middle-order batsman Gary Cosier first heard about the Centenary Test. When he later heard that the Queen was going to be watching part of the match, he knew it was a big occasion. Generally, the players didn't think the Test would be a big deal, although it meant a few would be playing their first Test against England and that meant a lot.

It wasn't just the players who were nervous leading into the match. Two days before the game the England batsman Keith Fletcher ventured too close to the centre strip and received a verbal blast from curator Bill Watt. Fletcher gave the strip a gentle prod with his bat and it was enough to upset Mr Watt, who was rolling practice wickets 80 metres away!

Even the mainstream press cartoonists were getting in on the act. In relation to all the tall stories, no doubt to be shared at the celebration with all the old timers getting together, a Frank and Ernest cartoon by Bob Thaves saw the two characters standing outside of the Scottish castle of

Loch Ness, one standing and wearing a kilt. They watch on as a small dragon-like lizard slithers past. Frank says to Ernie, 'Age Ernie, all tales grow with the telling.'

Whether this Test would be a match for tall tales or would survive on its own was soon to be discovered.

The Centenary Test was classified as an official contest between the two countries but not deemed to be an Ashes-deciding game, since it was not part of the usual five-or six-match format

Author Frank Tyson asked in the official Centenary Test program:

> *Will posterity therefore judge the Centenary Test as an elaborate pageant staged to celebrate the first quaint match between England and Australia in 1877? Will it be deemed pure nostalgia and remembrance of an era when colonial met the mother country on the cricket field in terms of equality and defeated her? Will it just be judged a ceremony recalling the days of Bannerman's 165, of brown cricket boots, spotted shirts and ties on the Test field?*

The match was initially being referred to in the mainstream as an exhibition match. Greg Chappell thought otherwise, 'Whenever you have Australia and England playing it's always a very tough contest.' And so it would prove to be.

There was also a sad note to the lead-up to the match with the passing of the former Chairman of the Queensland Cricket Association and Queensland delegate to the ACB, Frank Malone, who died after a long illness.

CHAPTER VIII

FROM INDIA WITH LOVE

England arrived in Australia via a tour of the subcontinent, exhausted from its heavy playing schedule. There was a lack of any real consideration for the players after a gruelling five-Test-match tour of India where they had to criss-cross the continent enduring all sorts of weather extremes, fitting in a packed schedule in sometimes challenging conditions.

Despite this England team manager, Ken Barrington, helped keep the team in good spirits with his 'can do' attitude as Mike Selvey later remembered:

> *Ken was the manager of the single tour that I had with England to India, Sri Lanka and Australia in the winter of 1976–77, a role he embraced with energy, enthusiasm, boundless optimism and humour, unable to pass up any invitation for the team to go to tea somewhere or to meet the local 'Mr Chief Minister'.*

Some of the England players would have been quite happy to have returned home after the tour of the subcontinent but Barrington, with his eager enjoyment of anything involved in touring and cricket, helped bring the doubters around.

Despite the conditions, the tour of India and Sri Lanka was really a matter of the tide turning for the England side. After comprehensive losses to the West Indies and Australia during home summers, for the first time in five outings England defeated India on home soil.

England captain Tony Greig was cock-a-hoop after leading England on his first tour as captain. He described his side's tour of India, in his book, *My Story*:

> *India had been conquered despite a scandalous character assault in Madras and almost laughable umpiring standards in Bangalore. The series ended 3–1 in England's favour and was a greater triumph than those at home could have possibly anticipated.*

John Lever was the player embroiled in controversy. His ability to swing the ball had been questioned, even more so when he was seen rubbing the ball over his eyebrows every now and then. Lever was accused of using Vaseline, placed above his eyebrows to stop the sweat dripping into his eyes, to shine the ball.

The name Derek Randall was just another on the list of young hopefuls chosen for the trip to India, Sri Lanka and Australia, the last to be made under the banner of the MCC. He was nicknamed Arkle, after the great steeplechaser, because he ran with those long bounding strides.

Off the field he was doubting and self-conscious. On the field he looked and behaved like a different character. Some of his act was a camouflage for his jangling nerves; a way of releasing tension. Once selected in the Tests Randall was unsure whether to continue clowning around on the field. Tony Greig, though, was adamant:

> *I told him to act the fool as he pleased because the crowd would love him for it—and if they were in good humour there would be little chance of trouble. Derek was off before the first ball had been delivered flicking his sun hat in the air and catching it on his head. Periodically, throughout what was a scorching day, he repeated his*

hat trick, somersaulted or slouched into an outrageous swaggering walk. It all set him up as an idol for the rest of the series.

Randall's naivety was also on show. Towards the end of the tour, a rich Bombay couple invited the players to their palatial beach house for a party. The food was exotic, too exotic for some of the players, including Randall. Not accustomed to champagne, toast and caviar Randall called across to his captain, 'Hey Greigy, the champagne's alright but the black currant jam on the toast tastes like fish!'

Randall like many of his team-mates was taken aback by what he saw. In his autobiography *The Sun Has Got His Hat On*, Randall admitted:

> *I had no idea what to expect in India…I had no conception of the staggering contrasts in climate, culture and landscape I was about to witness nor did I bother to find out such essential things as the need to be careful of the water in certain parts, to eat sensible food and to protect myself from the sun. Perhaps the thing that surprised me most was the impact our presence had on the public. We were treated as the nearest thing to royalty, garlanded everywhere we went and besieged by wide eyed young fans in the streets of every city…the Indians' enthusiasm for the game and hero worshipping of its players was something that will live with me forever.*

The great moment for the England captain Tony Greig arose at Calcutta's Eden Gardens where he scored a 347-ball three-day illness-affected and match-changing 103. England had bowled India out for 155 with the help of a heroic effort by Bob Willis with 5–27 from 20 overs.

By the end of the second day England in reply were 4–136 with Greig undefeated on 19. The next day Greig played before a crowd estimated between 80,000 and 100,000, which made a deafening noise with exploding firecrackers, while giant catapults made from the inner tubes of truck tyres projected oranges from the crowd right to the centre of the field. Mirrors flashed in the players' eyes. It was an intimidating environment for the visiting side. Former England bowler Mike Selvey, later writing in *The Guardian*, wrote of Greig's innings:

> *Greig played an innings of unwavering determination, self-denial and immense courage. The conditions alone—in which the ball was already spitting and turning sharply for Bedi, Erapalli Prasanna, Bhagwat Chandrasekhar—were wretched.*

When Greig returned to his hotel room that night he felt ill. He had caught a fever and became severely ill, shivering and sweating at the same time. He sweated so much he had to keep ringing room service to have the sheets changed. The team's physiotherapist Bernie Thomas was called and took Greig's temperature at 104 degrees. A hot bath and a change of bedding didn't help nor did sleeping pills. Eventually some medication from Thomas at 3am did.

On the third day, a square cut off Bishan Bedi saw England pass India's total. Greig gave one chance to Eknath Solkar at short leg on 33 but smothered Bedi by taking off-stump guard to minimise the risk of an edge as the ball turned away from him.

Just as he had taunted the Australian fast bowlers two summers before, he would gain the mental ascendancy by baiting India's bowlers. When Bedi defeated Greig with a quicker ball Greig would shout at the Indian captain, 'Come on 'Bish'', and 'Keep that arm straight.'

England scored only 147 runs all day, but, on a wicket that Greig viewed as not being up to Test standard after being scrubbed bare of grass, they lost only two wickets. Greig had batted all day to move from 19 to 94 and he used his height to advantage, smothering the ball.

After the rest day, where his health improved, Greig reached his century. Greig had scored only nine runs in the final session of the previous day and he reached his century in the first over of the fourth day, driving the ball to reach the milestone after 402 minutes at the crease.

After Greig was out for 103 England was dismissed for 321 and the rest of the day was a procession of Indian wickets. Amazingly, a crowd of 80,000 showed up on the final day, even though India was already seven wickets down.

Greig had endeared himself to the Indian public like few visiting captains before him. Whether it was by gestures like getting his players to put on their touring blazers and walk around the ground waving, or, if the game had started to drift Greig would encourage Derek Randall to turn some cartwheels. One time Randall, not playing in a match, assembled a squad of police, donned one of their hats and marched around the ground. Greig turned, at times what could have been a tricky situation, into one where he won the crowds over with slapstick acts such as clutching his cheek and staggering as if shot when a fire cracker went off.

Randall was relieved that England had fielded first, providing a chance to get used to the conditions. When he batted he made 37 but had trouble coping with the cacophony of noise.

Bedi was the crowd's idol and each time he glided up to bowl those tantalising left-armers, the roar would intensify until, at the moment of delivery, it was difficult to separate it in volume from the noise which greets a Cup-final goal at Wembley.

England keeper–batsman Richard Tolchard remembers the adulation of the crowds:

> *The Indian crowds loved us as much as their own teams. We never felt threatened, they had this rapport with Greigy and Randall. Greigy would blow kisses to the Ladies' stand. It was electric. Before games we would do our warm up laps round the outfield and they became laps of honour. We'd be talking to fans through the fences.*

Greig clearly had a positive effect on his players. A leader but also one who didn't see his players as subordinates.

John Lever recalled an incident where he and Greig had stayed at the ground after the first Test in Delhi to talk to the press. The remainder of the side had caught the team bus back to their hotel. The pair found themselves stranded at the ground and so, while still dressed in their whites, they hailed some passing motor scooters who took them back to their hotel—an incident that would surely not happen in the modern age!

Greig, having come off back-to-back series against Australia and then the West Indies at home, had clearly had enough of fending balls off his neck and throat:

> *The real delight of the Indian tour was in the opportunity to Test one's batting talents against the subtle skills of world-class bowlers...with no risk of injury.*

Greig, having been in the captain's role for just over eighteen months, was learning some of the challenges in leadership involved in trying to build up the confidence of his players—no easy feat for the likes of Greig who was naturally very confident and extroverted.

One player not so extroverted and confident was the England opener Dennis Amiss. He had experienced a torrid time at the hands of Lillee and Thomson just two summers before and what had happened was still fresh in his memory.

Dennis Amiss was clearly struggling with the prospect of having to face Dennis Lillee again, despite averaging more than 50 in India. Greig who had watched Amiss closely throughout the tour reflected on how, 'Amiss talked frequently of his problems against pace and it was clear to me, that for him, the real fight of the trip was to come at the end in Melbourne.' As Amiss later revealed, 'it was a matter of give up or keep going and I didn't much like the idea of giving up.'

Overall the trip to India was a great success: a 3–1 victory in the series highlighted by the strength of the wins, including, an innings and 25 runs and ten wickets and 200 runs. The MCC remained undefeated in eight other first-class matches, although only one was won.

Randall had learned some valuable lessons from the Indian experience, not the least of which was the need to use his feet to the spinners and to move out of his crease more. 'The biggest mistake I made in India was refusing to play the sweep shot. At home this stroke had been coached out of me.'

While pace rather than spin would be Randall's biggest challenge in Australia his reintroduction of the sweep shot would prove to be a handy skill during the Centenary Test.

PERTH

The itinerary for the visiting England side did them few favours. From the turning wickets of the sub-continent, they were scheduled to play Western Australia in Perth in a three-day match from 5 to 7 March on a hard bouncy WACA pitch prepared by Roy Abbott. To understand the challenge that this presented to the England side, fresh from the slow, turning wickets of India, one has to understand the nature of the WACA wicket.

Preparation time was also minimal. England arrived at 6am the day before their three-day match against Western Australia, after an eighteen-hour journey from Colombo via Singapore, where the visitors found they had to spend four hours in transit at Singapore Airport.

The WACA pitch had a reputation of being the fastest and bounciest strip in the world. Western Australian Shield player Ian Brayshaw, in his book *The Miracle Match*, could remember four players suffering a broken jaw when hit facing the quicks on the WACA track, namely Len Pavy (Western Australia), Ray Jordon (Victoria), Bob Cunis (New Zealand) and Max Walker (Victoria).

'It was at time, a truly vicious pitch', Brayshaw concluded. This was a time when helmets were not worn, or indeed arm guards and chest guards. In fact, the protective equipment consisted of flimsy pads, gloves and protectors to protect batsmen from a ball potentially travelling up to 160km per hour.

The WACA pitch stood out from other strips across the country and the world because of the soil used for the pitch. Harvey River soil.

The Harvey River, about 100km south of Perth, created massive clay deposits when the river flooded and the sedimentary overspill packed down to create a naturally hard surface. The dominant clay in these soils, smectite, swells when wet and contracts when drying out and sets very hard. This meant that the WACA pitch would be rock-hard and a surface that cracked. Curator Roy Abbot made a habit of using high magnesium (which tightened the soil) and smectite soil on his pitches. In the days when the WACA pitch was used only twenty days a year the surface had time to recover. The result though was a hard, baking WACA wicket. The Australians knew it and so too did visiting English teams.

It all meant that the English players, including opener Dennis Amiss, would face their nemesis yet again in ideal circumstances for Lillee. England in 1974–75 had a torrid time of it facing Jeff Thomson and Dennis Lillee on the hard bouncy pitches of Australia, none more than at Perth in 1974, where Australia won by nine wickets.

In a match that saw the debut of future Australian opening batsman Graeme Wood, Western Australia won the toss and batted. A first-day crowd that eventually totalled 11,222 saw Wood score 37 in 85 minutes with five fours. But it was the home side's middle-order batsman, Craig Serjeant, who scored a fine century of 101 in 226 minutes, (one six and nine fours) stroking the ball with great fluency. Kim Hughes chipped in with 39 in just under two hours, showing signs of restraint that he later appeared lacking. Rod Marsh collected 59 at a run a ball with some lusty hitting, as the home side accumulated 326.

The touring side had some trouble adjusting to the bounce of the WACA wicket. Amiss' horror run against Dennis Lillee continued when he was caught in the slips by Ian Brayshaw for nine. Brearley (61 in 199 minutes), Miller (56 in 131 minutes) and Barlow (60 in 126 minutes) consolidated, although, they were helped by the poor fielding by the home side, which dropped five chances. The likely top-order for England for the Centenary Test—Woolmer, Randall and Greig—all missed out.

With the help of Ric Charlesworth (69) and Rob Langer (83, ominously run out by Randall) WA set England 310 to win in 180 minutes plus 15 overs. Finishing on 8–239 England used the innings as batting practice. Brearley scored an undefeated 58 and Woolmer 51. Randall batted at number 3 and scored 31.

It wasn't the prefect preparation for the one-off Test match for the visitors. England fast-bowler Bob Willis had gone wicketless for 81 runs, as had Chris Old off just 11 overs. Mike Selvey who would miss out on selection for the Centenary Test took six wickets for the match (3–102) and (3–81).

Amiss fell to Lillee twice, making his average against Lillee in their past ten clashes 5.9, with Lillee picking him up eight times.

Pat Gibson of the *Daily Express* wrote:

> *Dennis Lillee looks like turning the Melbourne Centenary Test into war instead of a cricket celebration. Tony Greig declared a little later that 'If this is not a war, it will be the first Test I've played that hasn't been.'*

Gibson continued, 'Amiss, he claimed "suffered more abuse both physical and verbal than any cricketer should have to undergo".'

London's *Daily Mail* described Lillee as 'scoring another personal day of success…with the passable imitation of a bad tempered schoolboy.'

Amiss wasn't feeling too good himself, having been dispatched for just 9 and 29 runs in two innings against Western Australia at the WACA. Both times he was the victim of Lillee. 'The transformation from slow, low turning wickets in India to playing in Perth was not the start we wanted. It wasn't easy and was quite a good move by the Australians', Amiss observed.

The fact that the Centenary Test was being played on the seaming wicket of the MCG provided some consolation for Amiss, although the challenge he faced in fronting up to Lillee again was clearly enormous. 'Obviously Dennis got me out a few times and the thought was still in my mind.'

Looking back all these years later it must be hard for Amiss to recall the way he must have felt. He does however concede that, on reflection, he wished he had had more exposure to Australian wickets during the earlier years of his career:

> *I went to South Africa in my early career as a lot of us did to play and coach but I wished I had gone to Australia to play grade cricket and get used to the bounce of the wickets.*

The England team endured a four-hour flight from Perth to Melbourne, finding once they arrived that they had an unexpected escort to their hotel—a helicopter hovered over the bus all along the route.

It was only then, just a few days before the game, that England's players realised how big the match was going to be.

For Greig it was obvious once they arrived at the Hilton and saw some of the past greats like Larwood, Hutton, Compton, Edrich, Lindwall, Miller, Johnston and Hassett. Greig said, 'History was clustered with faces and voices from cricket's past…If you allowed yourself to be affected by it, you would soon be overpowered.' Somehow they needed to cut themselves off, play their game and yet at the same time be respectful to their predecessors. It was 'an occasion that belonged as much to them as it did to us'.

CHAPTER VIII

A SENSE OF CELEBRATION

The Centenary Test was in itself a celebration of the history of Anglo–
Australian Test cricket. More than 200 ex-players were present. Among
those to miss out was 89-year-old England great, Frank Woolley, on what
would have been his fourth tour to Australia. He was thwarted by age, with
his doctor advising against taking the long flight.

There were barbs among the celebrations. Len Hutton was busy ruffling
some Australian feathers with his words on arriving on Australian shores
that, 'You've got Dennis Lillee and Australian umpires.' Words that
would have caused the highly respected officials, Tom Brooks and Max
O'Connell, to baulk.

When Australia's premier fast bowler Dennis Lillee looked ahead to the
Centenary Test he couldn't help but notice the large number of official
functions. Lillee, like many of his team-mates, tired of such functions
where players would have to engage in small talk with sponsors and
cricket officials. The players might have enjoyed the free beers on offer
but generally wearied of the endless string of functions. However, Lillee
was pleasantly surprised by what the functions before the Centenary Test
match brought. He told Richie Benaud:

> *I can remember at one function there was everyone in this*
> *room, Bradman, Larwood, Lindwall, Miller and even Stork*
> *Hendry. There were all these players I had read about.*

*The feeling in the room was that you almost expected a
big bearded figure to walk in the room that was the feeling
talking to other players in the room.*

When Ian Davis was looking at his invite from the ACB to play in
the Centenary Test he couldn't help but notice the numbers of functions
associated with the match. He also noticed that the Queen was going to be
attending, adding weight to the match's significance. There was another
aspect that Davis found intriguing. 'They also asked us to bring our blazers.
We'd normally just turn up in civvies without blazers, which we never
really had to wear, so that meant it was a special occasion.'

For David Hookes, there were more lessons in the form of a rushed trip
back to an official function after he had arrived late when he woke late
from an afternoon nap and arrived not wearing a tie. He was then sledged
publicly by England captain Tony Greig at the cocktail party before the
match, 'Another left hander who can't bat', Greig spat out as he waltzed
by. Hookes looked around for Gilmour and Marsh, who were nowhere to
be seen. The youngster had had a tough initiation and the game hadn't even
started yet.

Gary Cosier described walking around the Hilton hotel as a surreal
experience:

*It was a matter of you didn't know who you were going
to bump into next. You'd see guys like Percy Fender and
Clarrie Grimmett and the more recent greats Truman and
Edrich. It was a bit like a party.*

Rod Marsh thought the scenes intimidating. 'Every time you go into the
hotel you see 200 blokes who are better cricketers than you.'

Australia's opening batsman, Rick McCosker, was just two years in to
a fledgling Test-cricket career. Unlike Greg Chappell's band of lovable
rogues, McCosker was reserved, shy even. As he caught his taxi from
Tullamarine airport to the Melbourne Hilton he reflected on the number of

former Australian players on his Ansett flight and the large signs strung up around city streets informing people of the Centenary match.

When we got there I noticed the City of Melbourne was humming as only Melbourne can do when there's a major sporting event on. We arrived a couple of days before the match and we tried to focus on practice but there was so much happening, functions, luncheons, dinners former players to talk to.

As he walked into the Hilton hotel, where both the Australian and England teams were staying, McCosker, who was known as the General (after General Custer), may well have pondered what a whirlwind the last two summers had been. A belated call up to the first-class game two weeks before he turned 27 was converted within months to Test selection.

Such was the pressure associated with the Centenary Test that England captain Tony Greig barred former players from the dressing room, 'There's more than 50 of them, and they all know more about cricket than any of us.'

Greig was also feeling the pressure from almost losing to Western Australia in the lead-up match. As the VIP guests were all settling down at their digs at the Hilton, Greig's side arrived from Perth. At the airport they met with the only mix-up of the entire Centenary schedule. Their aircraft arrived fifteen or so minutes early, catching the official welcoming party slightly unprepared.

Greig was on the front foot early saying at the press conference, 'It will be a sporting war...It will be a bloody great battle. There is no love lost in Tests between England and Australia.'

The Australian press had greeted Greig's men in Melbourne as a 'new look' team. Peter McFarline told his *Age* readers:

Most MCC touring teams have had a reputation in recent years for a dour approach to cricket and life, an uncommon dread of the press and something amounting

to a dislike of touring. But not anymore. Well not under
South African-born captain Tony Greig and manager Ken
Barrington.

McFarline had been very impressed by Greig's stated open press policy. 'You can talk as much as you like to any of the players at any time,' McFarline noted. 'This is a state of affairs that has not always existed.' Greig, leading England for the first time, was winning the public relations exercise.

One of the most celebrated visitors to Australia was the near-blind 84-year-old Percy Fender. Fender was the veteran of the English and despite his vision impairment and being wheelchair-bound he had a great time. His constant companion, who became his eyes, was his 13-year-old grandson Nicholas Bensted Smith, who lived in Melbourne. He pushed his grandfather's wheelchair around and described the details of the match. The teenager was constantly being reminded of how good a player his grandfather was, holding the fastest hundred ever scored in first-class cricket.

Christopher Forsyth, in his book *Pitched Battles: The History of Australia—England Test Cricket* described the City of Melbourne as:

> *The only big city that still reflects the image and aspirations*
> *of its transplanted English founders of 133 years ago,*
> *breathed in once again, like a middle aged lady preparing*
> *to lift her trailing skirts before stepping over a puddle.*

The annual Moomba festival was in full swing with Walt Disney's Mickey Mouse as its king and, of course, Melbourne society held high hopes about the impending visit of the Queen. The city of Melbourne was booked out for the duration, making it impossible to find accommodation during the week of the Centenary Test.

Leading English commentator John Arlott declared:

> *Cricket is Australia's most effectively aggressive form of*

nationalism...there's nobody to play Australian Rules with,
but at cricket they can rule the world roost and that must
be a tempting thing.

McCosker found that he didn't get much of a chance to talk to the older generation of players as they tended to keep to themselves.

When journalists Eric Beecher and Ken Piesse went behind the scenes of the Centenary Test they found that it was there that the match really happened. Described as a million-dollar operation and the most publicised event of all time, the Centenary Test was one that took over an entire luxury hotel and required a chartered aircraft to assemble a section of its central characters.

As Beecher and Piesse wrote in their article 'A Week at the Hilton' for the April edition of *Cricketer* in 1977:

Behind the scenes—in the grey anonymity of the Melbourne
Cricket Ground grandstands, in a hundred hotel rooms, in
the bars and buffet, and in the official viewing area—was
where this match really happened.

Featuring a cast rich in cricket history there were no fewer than eight former England captains—Hutton, Allen, Wyatt, Yardley, May, Smith, Dexter, Denness. Not to be outdone there were nine former Aussie skippers including Lawry, Johnson, Benaud, Craig, Hassett, Ryder, Simpson, Bradman and Ian Chappell. It was ten days of a true cricketing celebration.

Ted Dexter breezed in to Melbourne in typically grand style—and then breezed out again, leaving the Test celebrations one night, flying to Sydney to watch the Miracle Mile trotting experience at Harold Park, returning the next morning having covered his expenses. Dexter was also writing stories for the London *Sunday Mirror* on the Centenary Test and had heard how thousands of Sunday papers had to be pulped when late news about England's first-innings collapse superseded stories in the papers about how Australia had all but lost the Test.

Dennis Compton's reputation for absent-mindedness gained greater momentum when just before boarding the jumbo jet for Australia realised he had left his passport behind. It turned out to be in Cardiff where he had spent the previous day watching a rugby international between Wales and England. After a few frantic phone calls the passport was delivered just in time to allow Compton to board the plane. Compton would also later take out the prize as the only official guest who forgot to pay their hotel bill—which amounted to a few hundred dollars covering food, drink and incidentals throughout the week.

Compton though was in his element. 'I just love this Australian beer. And the food. And the cricket and meeting old friends. And the races.'

For Sir Leonard Hutton it was his first visit to Melbourne in 20 years. 'Although I've been back to Australia on numerous occasions since my last trip here as a cricketer in 1954–55 it's always been only to Sydney and Brisbane. My work with a light engineering firm has brought me here on business frequently, but never to Melbourne.'

Sir Leonard met many old friends and renewed acquaintances with 'the best steak in Australia' at the Victorian Club—the scene of Australia's biggest robbery last year—more than $1.3 million.

Norman Yardley, never far from his pipe, demanded on arrival to see what he described as the eighth wonder of the world, the MCG. He soon made the walk across the parks to the stadium he hadn't seen since 1947.

Alec and Eric Bedser dressed identically as ever, and were often walking side by side. 'We not only wear the same clothes, but we live next door to each other in the same street', said Alec, 'Really it's not a practical joke, it is just the way it happens to turn out.'

None of the English visitors were as busy as former fast bowler David Brown who was then a racehorse breeder who ran a thoroughbred stud in Worcestershire and managed to fit in two visits to the Melbourne races plus a look at the Newmarket yearling sales.

Political leaders were out in force at the event. Australian Prime Minister Malcolm Fraser, Opposition Leader Gough Whitlam and former Prime Minister Sir Robert Menzies led a long line of politicians and other guests attending the match at various stages. As well as current and ex-players there were a number of umpires invited to the Test as official guests including G Hele, T Smyth (Victoria), G Borwick, T Brookes, E Wykes (NSW), C Hoy, L Townsend, L Rowan (Qld), R Bailhache, G Cooper, A Cocks, C Egar, M McInnes, M O'Connell (SA) and A Mackley (WA).

The only Australian living in England who made the trip was Neil Hawke who lives in Nelson, Lancashire. On the trip out he managed to make it to his home city of Adelaide where he had a reunion with his seventeen-year-old daughter Janet, whom he hadn't seen for eight years.

There were a number of former England players now living in Australia who made the journey. They included Frank Tyson (coaching director of the Victorian Cricket Association), Peter Loader (a WA travel agent and broadcaster), Harold Larwood (retired in Sydney) Geoff Boycott (playing a season of Sydney Grade cricket) and Tony Lock from Perth.

Given the extent of the celebrations it was understandable that there were some minor casualties during the week long celebrations. Among them was former England Test batsman Bill Edrich who came down with an attack of gout during the Centenary Week.

'It must be something in the Australian beer" quipped Edrich who was still able to display a sense of humour.

Red faces of hangover victims were commonplace in the lobby of the Hilton hotel causing Edrich to comment in a humorous tone. 'We'll all be bloody well dead before this lot is over.' One of the test sponsors TAA had made provisions for such problems. All guests were furnished with 'survival kits' containing Alka-Seltzer, throat lozenges and sticking plaster. There was plenty of Australian beer, champagne and oysters (the most popular item consumed during the test) despite England opener Reg Simpson experiencing eight hours of stomach aches after eating some bad oysters.

The MCG press box was crammed fuller than it has been for a test match for more than a decade with writers from Australia and around the world.

From Fleet Street there were the usual press corps—Peter Laker,

(*Daily Mirror*) Alec Bannister (*Daily Mail*) Pat Gibson (*Daily Express*), Henry Blofeld (*The Guardian*), Christopher Martin-Jenkins (BBC) and Clive Taylor (*The Sun*) who came down with suspected hepatitis and on the final days of the match had to listen to the match on the radio from his hotel room. The great cricket commentator John Arlott had to be convinced to cover the match for the BBC (he had trouble with the hot climes). He agreed to do so just to spend 40 minutes a day behind the microphone. He did however manage to spent some hours tasting and buying wine (as well as being the cricket correspondent for the Guardian he was also the resident wine critic)

Also in the press box were several former Test players Richie Benaud, Jack Fingleton and Bill O'Reilly as well as Ian Chappell and Ashley Mallett.

The Melbourne Cricket Ground was dressed up. Plants and shrubs were moved in and placed around the members' area where the VIP's spent their time. Flags were draped everywhere and the members' area was adorned with scoreboard canvas name plaques of the men who made up 100 years of Anglo–Australian cricket history. The oldest original canvas was 87 years old; it had the name of SE Gregory, who first played against England in 1890.

Stalls to sell food, drink and souvenirs were spread throughout the ground. In the Members the outside practice area was turned into a continuous bar and the indoor nets were transformed into a dining room. Entertainment abounded with Army, Navy and Air Force bands, a cricket ball throwing competition hosted by Paul Sheahan among the activities.

The official organisers licensed some fifteen separate companies to make more than 60 Centenary Test products. The total cost of running the Centenary Test was estimated to be $1million. MCG ground staff of more than 200 on most days was on hand to man the turnstiles while the cleaning bill was estimated to be more than $20,000.

THE UMPIRES
Umpiring duties for the Centenary Test were awarded to South Australia's Max O'Connell and Tom Brooks from New South Wales.

Tom Brooks was the senior of the two and by 1977 had shown an ability to handle a crisis. His most dramatic Test was in Sydney in 1971 when Ray Illingworth led England from the field after bottles and cans were thrown at fast bowler John Snow. He and Lou Rowan told Illingworth that if he did not return, England would forfeit the Test. Illingworth led his men back and they won the Test and the Ashes. Brooks had also stood in all six Tests during Ian Chappell's epoch-making Ashes-winning summer of 1974–75.

Born in Paddington he was schooled at the Catholic St Charles' school in Waverley and then, after winning a scholarship, he attended Christian Brothers' Waverley College. He, like his umpiring partner in the Centenary Test, became an accountant, working for the PMG department. Brooks tall and broad shouldered, played first-grade for Waverley as a pace bowler before serving in the Second World War. He was picked for the representative match between Stan McCabe and Arthur Chipperfield's elevens, where he played alongside Bill O'Reilly, Cec Pepper and Stan Sismey.

He switched to the Manly Club, helping them win their first Sydney premiership with Keith Miller and Jimmy Burke. In 1949–50 he played sixteen first-class games for NSW, capturing 65 wickets at an average of 22. Brooks became a grade umpire in 1965 and was promoted to Shield duties two seasons later. Within three years he was a Test umpire.

In the 1970s, Brooks was like a father figure to Max O'Connell, who described him as a 'great gentleman and great umpire'.

Max O'Connell arrived at the world of Test umpiring after playing A-grade district cricket for ten years for Port Adelaide, where he kept wicket to Test bowlers Eric Freeman and Neil Hawke. O'Connell had developed a love of the game from the time he was in short pants. He was working on the scoreboard for Bradman's last game as an A-Grade cricketer for Kensington at Alberton:

> *I was paid a shilling for a day's work and as he [Bradman] left the dressing room I asked him for his autograph. He said to me that if I carried his cricket bag to the cars he*

would give me an autograph. He had a large brown, green
and gold bag that I struggled to get into the car and he
made good with his deal.

O'Connell's last game had been Greg Chappell's first in grade cricket He also played league football for the Magpies, mainly in the reserves but occasionally in the league side under the firebrand coaching style of Fos Williams.

An injury in his mid-twenties saw O'Connell, on the suggestion of Port Adelaide Cricket Club colleague Fred Godson, take up football umpiring. He shifted to umpiring at reserves then league level in the SANFL. All up the accountant at the SA electricity Trust umpired 162 league games (when they had just one umpire) and officiated in interstate games at the MCG and Subiaco in Victoria versus Western Australia clashes.

Cricket umpiring followed in 1967–68, as did an elevation from C grade to A grade in one season in district cricket for the South Australian Cricket Association. The rapid ascension continued when after just seven first-class matches O'Connell found himself umpiring the Fifth Ashes Test at the MCG in 1970–71. Perhaps the occasion got the better of him when he gave Australian opening batsman Keith Stackpole not out in the first over. O'Connell called over and turned to walk toward square leg and as a result missed the England wicketkeeper Alan Knott take the catch. He also warned Snow for intimidatory bowling later in the match. O'Connell and Brooke first umpired together in the sixth Test of the series in Adelaide. Brooke again had to deal with recalcitrant behaviour from an England player. This time it was the objections of opening batsman Geoff Boycott who stood hands on hip and hesitated before he walked off after being run out by Ian Chappell and given his marching orders by Greg Chappell.

Surprisingly, O'Connell's appearances at Test level were spasmodic with him not even umpiring one Test during the 1974–75 Ashes series (umpired by Tom Brooks and Robin Bailhache). O'Connell was informed of his appointment to umpire the 1977 Centenary Test the week before the match:

*I had a phone call at work from ACB secretary Alan Barnes
at 9pm on the Friday night. I then had to wait until Monday
morning to ask my boss for ten days off.*

The late notice was due to the fact that both captains had to agree to the umpires, and the England team's arrival in Perth from India was delayed. O'Connell had little trouble convincing his boss, the former league footballer and district cricketer Roy Colyer, to agree to let him have some time off work: 'I couldn't believe my luck to be chosen to this match. It was the ultimate and the best thing that has happened to me.'

CHAPTER IX

THE MCC XI

Twenty-four players were selected to be part of this great celebration of Anglo–Australian cricket. England was captained by Tony Greig and included Bob Woolmer, Mike Brearley, Derek Underwood, Derek Randall, Dennis Amiss, Keith Fletcher, Alan Knott, Chris Old, John Lever and Bob Willis. Graham Barlow would carry the drinks for the visitors.

The South African-born England captain Tony Greig was at the zenith of his powers in 1977. He had made his name with Sussex and England as one of the fiercest competitors in cricket. He was a hard-hitting number-six batsman and change medium-pace or off-spin bowler.

Australian cricket fans knew him well from his success against Australia in 1974–75. His audacious ton in the first Test of the series against the might of Lillee and Thomson earned him a legion of fans on both sides of the cricketing fence. Greig's ability to rile the Australians was obvious at the Gabba when he struck 110 as he taunted the opposition bowlers by signalling fours with an exaggerated flourish each time he hit a boundary. Greig's career was mired in controversy during the English summer of 1976 when he struggled against the West Indies after promising the Caribbean tourists he would make them grovel. Coming from a South African, the comments were seized upon by the West Indies as motivation to ensure that they not only defeated England but dominated them. Greig had redeemed himself when he won over the Indian cricketing public scoring a seven-hour hundred at Calcutta in 1976 while keeping the crowd entertained in the process. He wooed the 80,000 plus crowd and they loved his antics. That type of adulation eased the path for his team as they travelled around the sub-continent. Under his leadership England won the series 3–1.

Greig took over the captaincy from Mike Denness in 1975 and by the time of the Centenary Test- had played 52 Tests scoring 3314 runs at an average of 41 with eight centuries

Mike Brearley, the 34-year-old vice-captain, was just one year into his Test career. He had taken a circuitous and lesser known path to Test cricket. From 1968 to 1970, he played only half a season of cricket in the London borough of Harrow. He first appeared for Cambridge as a 19-year-old in 1961 scoring 76 against Surrey and scores of 73 and 89 against Benaud's visiting Australians. He was also first choice wicketkeeper. In 1964, after a century against Bobby Simpson's Australians, Brearley appeared to have the cricketing world at his feet when he toured South Africa but had limited success.

Brearley captained England's under-25 team to Pakistan in 1966–67 scoring 793 for the tour and averaging 132. He played no cricket in England in 1966 and 1967 when pursuing an academic career at British and American universities. He returned to captain Middlesex in 1971, helping to steer a talented but until then rudderless ship in the right direction, winning the championship in 1976 and 1977.

Brearley made his Test debut against the West Indies in 1976, almost a decade after he had led the under-25 side to Pakistan. By the start of the Centenary Test he had played just seven Tests scoring 285 runs at 23 with a highest score of 91 on the 1977 India tour. When Brearley batted, he held his bat aloft before the bowler delivered the ball He was more of a nudger and deflector than hard striker of the ball.

Dennis Amiss historically struggled against Australia. As he told English *Cricketer* in October 2015:

> *I just never got going against Australia. In my first*
> *Test against them I got a pair. It was at Old Trafford*
> *in 1968. England lost by 159 runs and I didn't play*

another Test for three years. I never really recovered from that bad start.

At 33 years of age, England's opening batsman had seen the highest of highs in Test cricket and the lowest of lows. In 1974 he scored 1379 runs at an average of 68.95, failing by just two runs to break Bob Simpson's record number of Test runs in a calendar year. Amiss had his confidence shattered against Lillee and Thomson in 1974–75, finishing with three ducks in a row, all against Dennis Lillee. He reflected on that difficult time in his book *In Search of Runs*:

> *It was my third nought in successive Test innings. They had all lasted less than one over and at that stage I confess Lillee had built up a massive psychological stranglehold over me.*

He triumphantly returned to Test cricket in 1976 scoring 203 and 16 against the West Indies at the Oval. He then amassed 417 runs at an average of 52 against India.

For Amiss the Centenary Test would be an examination without parallel; rarely had a player failed in such a spectacular manner against the same opposition or, indeed, the same bowler. Amiss had proved against the West Indies that he could play against the pace that a bowler such as Lillee could generate. The challenge was a mental one—whether or not Amiss could stare down his fears against Lillee on the MCG in front of a parochial Australian crowd. By the time of the Centenary Test Amiss had played in 47 Tests hitting 3501 runs at 47.8 with a highest score of 262 against the West Indies in 1975–76.

Right-handed Nottinghamshire batsman, Derek Randall, had been brought up to play the way of the great West Indian all-rounder Garry Sobers—playing hard but fair and, most importantly, entertaining the crowd. While Randall had a love of the game from an early age, he never thought he'd be good enough to play professional cricket. When he was still in short pants Randall would turn up to his local club at Retford when they were short and field all day and have the occasional bat and bowl. By the time he was 13 he was in Retford's first team. It would later be the number that haunted the superstitious right-hander, who developed such a dislike for 13 when batting that he would occasionally get stalled on the number for extended periods attempting to ensure he wasn't dismissed for 13.

He was fortunate that Mike Hall, the Retford captain, was also the captain of the Notts second 11:

> *It was quite late when I made my debut for the Notts first team (in 1972). At Newark I was 21 a mechanical draughtsman at the time. I was so nervous. Garry (Sobers) batted me at number seven. Garry had about 50 so when I came in to bat the sting had come out of the Essex attack.*

If that wasn't intimidating enough, Randall had been overawed when he first set eyes on the Melbourne Cricket Ground. He had debuted against India only four Tests earlier at Eden Gardens in Calcutta, where at least 80,000 packed the stands each day of the match. He still managed to hold his nerve and score 37 in his side's ten-wicket win. Randall struggled to convert starts throughout the tour and by the time the MCC arrived in Australia it was uncertain as to whether he or Graham Barlow would play in the Centenary Test. In four Tests in India he had scored only 86 runs at 12.28.

England's wicketkeeper, Alan Knott, had a reputation as the best keeper in the world. Small and nimble behind the stumps and prone to performing a series of stretching exercises in between deliveries, he was also superstitious, choosing to touch the bails in between deliveries. In the ten years up to the Centenary Test Alan Knott played 89 of England's 93 Tests, nearly twenty more than any other Englishman. As a batsman he put a high price on his wicket. In only his fourth Test, at Georgetown in

1967–68, he made 73 not out in four hours and helped Colin Cowdrey save the series. In 1974–75 he was one of the few English batsman to stand up to the pace attack of Lillee and Thomson in Australia, scoring a century in the Fifth Test at Adelaide. A season later he defied the barnstorming West Indian attack at home to score a century at Trent Bridge.

Cricket was in Knott's blood from an early age. He had started watching his father Eric, who was a wicketkeeper for the Belvedere CC, from the age of four. His dad was also the goalkeeper for the Erith Council in the South London Alliance League, which may explain some of the goal-saving moves that Knott later developed when keeping for England. Knott used to score for the Belvedere CC first side and got his first game of cricket when the second 11, playing on the adjacent pitch against the City of London College, were one short. It was 1957 and Knott was 11 years old.

Knott practised catching a tennis ball at home with his elder brother Francis. They played with stumps and it was here that Knott first began that ability of anticipating where the ball would go off the stump, a crucial skill for wicketkeepers.

The same year, Knott's history teacher Jack Morris, who also looked after the school cricket teams, offered him the chance to go to the Eltham indoor nets where Kent also trained. Knott went as an opening batsman and bowler and soon caught the attention of the head coach Claude Lewis. Former England batsman–keeper and then Kent Manager, Les Ames, was also there, soon setting Knott the challenge of a sixpence every time he was able to dismiss David Constant the former Kent batsman and later one of England's leading umpires.

It wasn't until Knott was 15 and wicket keeping for Kent schools that Ames saw Knott's potential as a gloveman. He continued to develop as a keeper and at the age of 16, while still at school, played for the Kent Club and Ground side and the second 11 during school holidays. He went on an International Cavaliers tour to Jamaica and Barbados in 1964–65 when he was 18 and his heroes Godfrey Evans, Fred Trueman, Trevor Bailey, Jim Laker and Ken Barrington also attended. Any thought he had of becoming a teacher was supplanted by a desire to play cricket for a living. When

Kent's wicketkeeper moved to South Africa in 1964 Knott began his lengthy career as a keeper for his county.

An under-25 tour with England/MCC to Pakistan in 1966–67 saw Knott not only excel with the gloves, with 11 catches and 11 stumpings, but also perform solidly with the bat scoring 326 at 36, including a 101 versus North Zone at Peshawar. A Test debut against Pakistan arrived in August of 1967.

He told the *Wisden Cricketers' Almanack* in September of 2008:

> *Playing cricket showed me what it was like to be fit and healthy and how lucky we were to be paid and trained athletes and to be looked after by some of the best trainers and medical and treatment staff in the country.*

Knott was one of the most diligent when it came to fitness and preparedness for matches. Lean and lithe behind the stumps, Knott moved in a minimalist way and then would spring cat-like, suddenly, to take a dramatic catch. In 1977 he was at the peak of his powers.

For Keith Fletcher the 1974–75 England tour to Australia must have seemed like a recurring nightmare. He was one of the front line English batsmen who struggled to come to terms with the pace of Lillee and Thomson. He made some amends with a score of 146 in the sixth and final Test at the MCG against an attack minus Thomson and Lillee (who went off injured after three overs). Fletcher struggled against the pace, often stepping back towards square leg, and at one time being struck on the St George dragon of his cap.

By the time of the 1977 Centenary Test Fletcher had scored 2970 runs at 41.25, including seven centuries in 51 Tests, but with only one against Australia. His highest score was 216 against New Zealand in 1974–75. He had struggled in India scoring just 91 runs at 22.

The Australians appeared to have a certain disdain for Keith Fletcher. Although other batsmen in history had used a backing away approach to success, Fletcher had tried it and failed. His efforts in 1974–75 more resembled a batsman who didn't want to get in line behind the ball than one with a definite strategy. Although various batsmen over the years had tried it successfully, generally speaking, backing away from the line of the delivery opens the batsman up to all sorts of criticism about his courage. To be seen as lacking in courage as a batsman is as harsh a criticism one can offer. Fletcher was fortunate to be included in the side after a disappointing tour on the spin-friendly pitches of the sub-continent that favoured his front-foot technique.

One of England's new faces, the tallish fair haired and lithe John Lever, had amazing success on first tour of India. He played county cricket for Essex for ten years before getting an England cap. Twenty-six wickets at 14 headed the averages for both sides. A left-arm medium seamer, Lever had the ability to angle the ball across a right hander and also bring the ball back in, trapping many an unsuspecting batsman LBW. A high level of fitness and an ability to bowl long spells in difficult conditions made Lever an effective workhorse bowler as well as one who could create a dynamic spell early in the innings. He proved immediately that he was able to adapt to the pressures of Test cricket when on his first active day in test cricket he made 53 and took 4 for 16 in his opening spell, deceiving the Indian batsmen with his late in swing.

Chris Old was a right-arm fast bowler and left-hand bat. He had played 30 Tests scoring 620 at 16 and taking 90 wickets at 29.87. Old's best performance was 5–21 against India in 1974. More at home in English conditions where he could swing the ball, at times with great menace, Old struggled on his previous trip to Australia in 1974–75.

Old was also a powerful left-handed batsman who, in 1977, scored what was then the third fastest first-class century in 37 minutes against Warwickshire. He was also brilliant in the field, sharp in the slips and athletic in the deep. For Old, his worst enemy was his injuries. Operations on both knees in 1970 and 1971 affected his confidence and he also suffered frequently from strains in the shoulders or the side. He played in four Tests in India in 1977 scoring 95 runs at 15.83 and took ten wickets at 20.10. Ninety wickets at 29 from 30 Tests proved his effectiveness at

Test level

At 31, Derek Underwood was the best left-arm orthodox spinner in the world and third highest in his country's list of wicket takers with 248 wickets at 24. Known as 'Deadly', Underwood's pace was slow medium but he was able to vary his pace and flight skilfully. He first played for Kent when he was 17 and became the youngest player to take 100 wickets in his first season.

He took some time to become as effective a bowler overseas as he was in England because of a reluctance to give the ball greater flight when it was required. On occasions he was a match winner; there was no better example than when he took 7–50 against Australia in 1968 at The Oval.

Underwood's best performance of 8–51 was against Pakistan in 1974. Having toured Australia twice, he didn't gain the same success that he had at home on softer wickets. Against India in 1977 he took 29 wickets at 17.55.

Bob Willis, a 198cm frizzy-haired opening bowler for England debuted against Australia in 1970–71 when he flew out to replace Alan Ward. Willis gave an indication of his strong personality when he returned home and controversially left his county of Surrey for Warwickshire after the county had been unwilling to give him a county cap (when a player becomes recognised and established for a club). Running in off a long run, Willis' open-chested action made him awkward to face. Capable of a mean bouncer and a penetrating yorker, he bowled with courage and consistency on his second tour of Australia in 1974–75 taking 17 wickets at 30.70. His 5–42 against the powerful West Indies side of 1976 on a good Headingley pitch again proved his worth while 20 wickets at 16.75 in five Tests in India showed he could adapt to the conditions. In 26 tests he had taken 76 wickets at 24.47 with a best of 6–53 against India in 1976–77

Bob Woolmer was an all-rounder from Kent who was born in Kanpur and lived in India until the age of seven. He first played for his county in 1968 and was capped two years later. In 1975 he took a hat trick for the MCC against the Australians and later debuted in the Lord's test of the summer with scores of 33 and 31. Later that summer he made 149 to save the Oval Test of 1975, reaching the slowest century for England against Australia in six hours 36 minutes. Woolmer struggled against the West Indies in 1976 and in India in 1976–77 (he played only two Tests in India scoring 42 runs at 14). He had scored 505 runs at 31 and taken nine wickets at 89 in nine tests. Despite the figures, Woolmer was a solid batsman who could display graceful stroke play.

England's twelfth man, Graham Barlow, was a solid left-hander who had played for Middlesex since 1969. He'd made rapid improvement in 1976–77 when he scored 1478 runs at an average of just under 50, often in a quick manner. This performance had a lot to do with Middlesex's first outright Championship win since 1947. An unbeaten 80 against the West Indies in a one-day international had helped Barlow gain selection on the 197677 tour of India where he scored hundreds in his first two innings. Despite the promise, in two Tests in India Barlow only scored 11 runs at 5.50.

CHAPTER X

THE AUSTRALIAN XI

The Australia team, led by Greg Chappell, consisted of Ian Davis, Rick McCosker, Gary Cosier, David Hookes, Doug Walters, Rod Marsh, Gary Gilmour, Kerry O'Keeffe, Dennis Lillee, Max Walker and Ray Bright as twelfth man.

At age 28, Greg Chappell was Australia's premier batsman but felt he was coming to the end of his Test career. Following in the footsteps of brother Ian, Greg debuted at the age of 18 for South Australia against Victoria in the opening game of the 1966–67 season scoring 53 and an undefeated 62. A century against Queensland at the Gabba helped him finish with a respectable 501 runs at 35. Timely advice from Sir Donald Bradman about changing his grip (with the top hand placement moved more around the back of the handle) helped open his off-side play.

At the end of the 1967–68 season Chappell took off to play County cricket with Somerset after John Inverarity withdrew from the team when he was picked in the 1968 Australian side. Back home, in 1969–70 Chappell dominated with 856 at 65 and toured New Zealand with the Australian second 11. After a nervous start, he scored a century on debut against England in the second Test at Perth in 1970–71, the sixth Australian to achieve the feat, figuring in a stand with Redpath of 219. Having started his career with South Australia, he transferred to Queensland in 1973.

In 45 Tests he had scored 3684 runs averaging 55. A classical batsman with orthodox technique, Chappell had dominated the world's bowlers since arriving on the Test scene. His highest score was an undefeated 247 in 1973–74. Greg Chappell had taken over the captaincy of the Australian side from his brother Ian in 1975–76 and, since then, had won seven out of 11 Tests: 'I was winding down from Test cricket. The tour to England in 1977 was going to be my last. And I was ready to retire after that.'

One of the big personalities of the Australian side, Rod Marsh was one of Australia's leading wicketkeepers. When he first played for Western Australia it was as a batsman and he made a century on debut against the West Indies in Perth in 1968–69.

He had debuted for Australia in the Ashes series of 1970–71. Sections of the media who favoured Brian Taber cruelly gave Marsh the moniker 'iron gloves' but it didn't take long for Marsh to live this down. In the Fifth Test, Marsh accepted the decision of captain, Bill Lawry, to declare with Marsh on 92 not out, just eight runs short of what would have been his maiden Test century, helping Marsh to win over the knockers. He became Australia's first wicketkeeper to score a century in a Test when he made 118 against Pakistan in 1972–73 and his highest score was 132 against New Zealand in 1973–74.

The driving force of the Australian cricket team in the field, Marsh would cajole his team-mates into putting in that extra effort.

Marsh was the perfect foil for the fast bowling of Dennis Lillee. He was quick on his feet with superb judgement and anticipation enabling him to cover ground quickly. His acrobatic dives, strong appeals and habit of throwing the ball into the heavens after catching it all made him a favourite with crowds. Caught Marsh bowled Lillee became a catch phrase during the 1974–75 summer against England when Australia defeated the visitors 5–1. A hard-hitting batsman by the time of the Centenary Test, he had scored 2092 runs at 32 in 46 Tests.

Australia's fast bowler Dennis Lillee was like a force of nature—he was the most potent and electrifying figure in world cricket. Lillee was quick with a lethal bouncer aimed at the throat or head. He would also get down on his haunches and appeal in an exaggerated manner and then with an elongated sweep of his hand wipe sweat off his brow.

He debuted for Western Australia against Queensland in November of 1969 taking just three wickets but impressing astute judges. His debut season saw Lillee snare 32 wickets at 22 and selection in an Australian second team to New Zealand followed.

Lillee was like a professional in a semi-professional era and took every opportunity to do the extra work required. He was also driven by the advice of his maternal grandfather, Len Halifax, who told him, 'If you can get your second wind and be in control of your body, then your mind will be free to cope with the job ahead.'

Lillee took five wickets on debut against England in the Sixth Test against England in 1970–71 at Adelaide Oval. He developed a reputation for being a firebrand in England in 1972 when he led the way for Australia taking 31 wickets in the five-Test series.

His ability to swing and cut the ball at great pace and in a controlled manner was critical to Lillee's success. Having made an amazing comeback after a serious back injury in the West Indies in 1973 Lillee, along with Jeff Thomson, helped destroy the England batting line up of 1974–75. He became part of popular Australian culture by dint of his bowling abilities but also his theatrics on the field.

In his 31 Tests since 1970–71, Lillee had taken 160 wickets at 24 with a best performance of 6–66 against England in Manchester in 1972. By the start of the Centenary Test Lillee appeared to have an almost mesmerising effect on his opponents.

Doug Walters was a junior prodigy. Born in the New South Wales country town of Dungog, Walters was the classic case of a boy from the bush doing well. He celebrated a first-class debut at the age of 17 with a score of 50 against a Queensland attack led by the West Indian speedster Wes Hall.

In 1964–65 his all-round abilities were evident when he scored 253 for New South Wales against South Australia and took 7–63 with his gentle outswingers. Two weeks before his twentieth birthday he scored 155 on Test debut against England in 1965–66 at Brisbane but had been unable to replicate his home form in England when he toured in 1968, 1972 and 1975.

National service interrupted his test development where he missed the 1966–67 tour of South Africa. He made a successful return against the West Indies in 1968–69. Appearing in only four of the Tests he scored at a 'Bradmanesque' rate with scores of 76, 118, 110, 50, 242 and 103.

Moderate success though followed against the South African attack of 1969–70 and John Snow's England team in 1970–71. On three occasions he scored 100 in a single session of a Test (against the West Indies in 1973, New Zealand in 1973–74 and England in 1974–75). New Zealand felt the full brunt of his attacking style when he scored 250 at Christchurch in 1976–77.

An inability to handle the seaming delivery and a habit of playing across the line saw him picked up cheaply in English conditions. On his day he was unstoppable and had also taken 49 wickets at 27 with deceptive medium-pace bowling. Walters, at age 32, was the fourth-most prolific Australian batsman in history after Bradman, Harvey and Lawry with 4667 runs at 50.17 in 62 Tests.

To arrive at the Centenary Test had been a long trip for the quietly spoken and reserved, right-hand opening batsman, Rick McCosker. Inverell born and bred, McCosker grew up in the northern New South Wales town on the McIntyre River, about 670km north of Sydney. He spent his early childhood, on the family sheep property 50km out of town. When a teenage McCosker scored three centuries in a row for Mount Russell in the Inverell District competition he put away the keeping gloves that he had so cherished as a young boy. McCosker's grandfather and father had both made a name for themselves in the country and McCosker wanted to follow in their footsteps. He could turn a mean leg spinner but preferred the feel of willow in his hand.

McCosker also excelled at tennis and played in the Country Championships at White City in Sydney. There came a moment when he had to decide between the two. Cricket won.

When he turned twenty he was transferred by his company, the Rural Bank, to Sydney, helping him to play grade cricket and push for state honours. He began at the Sydney club in the third grade, pushing his way into first grade during the season. In 1972–73 he made 48 for New South Wales colts against Victoria and finished second in the Sydney grade averages with 565 runs at 40.

A score of 13 on debut against South Australia in November 1973 and an undefeated 71 against Western Australia helped consolidate his place in the New South Wales side. 346 runs at 49 in that first season established McCosker as a steady if not exciting middle order batsman. The next summer, when he was moved up from the middle order to number three, proved a watershed moment. Two battling half centuries against the MCC showed McCosker's resilience while twin centuries (138 and 136 not out) against the might of Western Australia, led by Dennis Lillee, revealed his class.

In his Test debut against England in 1975 McCosker made a first innings score of 80 at the SCG in front of 50,000-strong home crowds. Even being struck on the head fielding in close couldn't dampen the newcomer's enthusiasm. By 1977 he had scored 1214 runs at 50.58 in 16 Tests.

The Centenary Test was notable for many things but especially for the arrival of the baby-faced South Australian batsman, David Hookes.

The summer of 1976–77 was the fulcrum on which the young left-hander's life turned in a dramatic way. It could easily have been very different. In just his second season of first-class cricket, Hookes had missed South Australia's eastern states tour in the second half of November, repeating his matriculation as an adult student at Marryatville High School.

A double failure in Perth against WA saw him under pressure to retain his place. Feeling a little unconfident when he arrived at the crease in an A-grade match against Prospect, he received the first of what would be a number of lucky breaks. Medium-pacer Bob May dropped a dolly caught-and-bowled chance off Hookes, who hadn't reached double figures. Hookes made the most of the miss and plundered a quick-fire 79. Five centuries in six innings for Hookes began with 163 against Victoria on 4 February and finished 16 days later with 156 against New South Wales.

There he was that night after stumps, Australia's latest Test selection, sweeping his longish hair back and looking a little shell shocked as he described the run to ABC TV: 'Yeah I've had a bit of a purple patch, it was just one of those things that happen when you have a good run.'

He couldn't have been more understated if he'd tried. Only Everton Weekes had hit five centuries in successive innings (1955–56), while Charlie Fry (1901), Sir Donald Bradman (1938–39) and Mike Procter (1970–71) hit six successive tons.

Just 21 years of age, he was on his way to play in what was being described as the biggest cricket match in one hundred years. When he arrived in Melbourne for the Centenary Test Hookes soon learned that he was an easy butt of practical jokes when his roommate, Gary Gilmour, told him to avoid the tramlines on Wellington Parade in order to avoid getting a nasty shock from the live lines. He also quickly learned to show respect to the senior players when Lillee refused to pick the ball up in the nets when Hookes batted it back to him.

For Greg Chappell the arrival of David Hookes into the Australian team was nothing new:

> You had players coming and going all the time. He was obviously a youngster with a reputation as a rising superstar, but I'd seen all this before. This was a big Test but so are all of them...the match has probably become bigger with hindsight really.

The day before the match started Ray Wilkins wrote a front-page profile of David Hookes for *The Australian* that showed the young left-hander standing next to Sir Donald Bradman (it was Bradman who wrote a letter to his friend and Australian selector Sam Loxton, encouraging Hookes to be selected). Hookes looked more like a pop star member of the band Sherbet than an Australian cricketer. He'd dressed in a leather jacket and open-neck shirt and was shaking hands with a bespectacled Bradman in a suit and tie. Although we didn't know it at the time, it represented a symbol of change from the old to the new that was about to reverberate around the cricketing world.

Greg Chappell knew that Hookes was in the mix to play:

There was a strong feeling that he would be in the touring team to England so it didn't come as a great surprise that he came into the side for the Centenary Test. There was a lot of talk about his run scoring late in the season.

When asked how he felt after such a golden run of five hundreds in six innings followed by his selection in the Australian side for such a historic match, Hookes replied:

People keep telling me about the law of averages but I've never been overawed in important matches. I'm nervous now that I've arrived in Melbourne, but I think everyone gets nervous like that.

Hookes had actually played three innings since the last of his six hundreds. He had been dismissed first ball in a charity match in Brisbane, and scored 10 and 12 in two innings for West Torrens. The way he saw, it the law of averages was about to swing back his way.

Hookes' only experience in front a large crowd was when he had seven goals kicked on him for West Torrens in an under-19 grand final in 1973 in one of the curtain raisers to the league premiership match where 56,525 eventually crammed in to the Adelaide Oval.

Australian leg spinner Kerry O'Keeffe played his cricket intensely. He had toured India with a schoolboys' team in 1966–67 and within two years made his debut for New South Wales at the age of 19. His action was ungainly and he would run to the wicket with his arms flailing before dropping his left arm prematurely in the delivery stride. However, taking 6–49 against Victoria in Sydney in 1969–70 confirmed his promise, earning him selection against England the following season. He took 3–48 and 3–96 in the seventh Test at Sydney. O'Keeffe then enjoyed a successful season at Somerset taking 77 wickets but missed the 1972 tour of England

and had a lean second season for Somerset.

1973 began with O'Keeffe attending an Advanced Coaches' certificate at the second Rothman's Sports foundation seminar. During an evening's relaxation it was decided to show footage of the West Indian captain, Garry Sobers, hitting 254 against Australia for the Rest of the World. O'Keeffe, while wondering at the magnificence of Sobers, saw a flaw in his own action. He was bowling too wide of the crease; his arm action was so high it was coming around behind his head; his follow through was finishing between his knees instead of beside and beyond his left knee. He suddenly realised why his team-mates were teasing him about his straight break:

> *There's no way I could bowl a leg break with that action. I'm bowling closer to the stumps I'm running in straighter, I've cut out the flailing arms just before delivery and I've cut out that leap. Basically I've likened leg spinning to the outswing bowler. They bowl close to the stumps, they take their follow through down their left side. It's the same principle...and the ball's turning from the leg.*

Touring the West Indies in 1973 he enhanced his reputation with several valuable performances. At Port of Spain his 4–57 was critical in Australia's narrow win over the West Indies. Back home, he hit his highest Test score of 85 against New Zealand in Adelaide. After two years away from Test cricket he bowled well against Pakistan and New Zealand taking 5–101 at Christchurch to earn his way into the side for the Centenary Test.

Gary Gilmour was the type of cricketer who looked like he was better suited to playing grade or even suburban cricket but was, in fact, a match-winning all-rounder at Test level. Round-faced and slightly overweight, he could strike the ball with ferocity and could swing the ball sharply as a brisk fast-medium bowler. He was unlucky to have played in an era when there were so many gifted Australian bowlers. Gilmour was a natural cricketer who only started playing competitive cricket in Newcastle, on the central coast of NSW when he was 12 years old. Although tennis and rugby league also appealed, cricket soon won out and was encouraged by his school coach Jack Finlay.

Gilmour played for Bob Simpson's side, Western Suburbs, and, as a 20-year-old, took 6–4 against Gordon in the first-grade final. A year later he did much the same to Gordon in a semi-final, capturing 8–75 including four wickets in four balls. By then he had already made a stunning debut for New South Wales scoring 122 (from 136 balls in 153 minutes, with one six and 19 fours, including a hundred in the session between lunch and tea), against South Australia. Gilmour had come into the side with the absence of John Benaud (Richie Benaud's younger brother), Kerry O'Keeffe, and Doug Walters for New South Wales, which was playing an opposition weakened by the loss of Greg Chappell, Ian Chappell Ashley Mallett and Ashley Woodcock, all of whom were playing for Australia against the Rest of the World at Adelaide Oval. New South Wales lost but it had unearthed a new star.

Two years later Gilmour debuted for Australia hitting 52 and taking 4–75 against New Zealand at Melbourne. Gilmour was surprised at the sense of high jinks in the Australian dressing room:

> *I was totally amazed about what went on in the first morning of a Test match in the dressing room...Keith Stackpole and Paul Sheahan went out to bat and 'Stacky' came back and ducked his head in the dressing room and said, 'You blokes to the races, you don't need to be here, these blokes can't play.'*

Keith Stackpole scored 122 out of Australia's total of 462.

In his last Test of the trans-Tasman series of 1973–74, Gilmour took 5–64 in the first innings at Auckland to help level the series at one all. Surprisingly, he did not appear for Australia in the 1974–75 Ashes series and did not play for Australia in the 1975 World Cup until the semi-final against England, where he took 6–14 from 12 overs. He was a regular team member of the Australian side that defeated the West

Indies in 1975–76, taking 20 wickets at 20.30 and hitting 95 in the Adelaide Test.

In 1976–77 he suffered from a nagging foot injury and managed only ten wickets in Tests against Pakistan and New Zealand. He did, however, make his maiden Test century at Christchurch, where he shared a stand of 217 in 187 minutes with Doug Walters. If anything, when the Centenary Test rolled around he looked like he was at the peak of his powers.

Max Walker had moved to Melbourne from Tasmania in 1967, chasing the dream of a VFL career with the Melbourne Football Club. He also joined the Melbourne Cricket Club. He gave the footy dream away five years later and concentrated on medium-pace bowling. Cricket success arrived immediately with Walker taking 85 wickets at 17, earning him a Victorian cap in 1968–69. He developed as an in swing bowler to one who could bowl a lethal leg cutter. Consistent performances with the ball earned him a baggy green against Pakistan in 1972–73, where he took five wickets. A week later his return of 6–15 denied Pakistan the easy target of 159. Walker's 26 wickets at 20.73 helped Australia to a 2–0 series win against the West Indies in 1973.

Known as 'Tangles' for his tangle-footed approach to the crease when bowling, Max Walker was a right-armed medium-paced bowler who had taken 119 wickets at 26 in 28 Tests including 8–143 against England in 1974–75. He was the first Tasmanian player to represent his country since Jack Badcock in 1936–37. He was also a valuable lower-order batsman scoring 425 runs at an average of 18.

Australia's twelfth man, Ray Bright, was a left-arm orthodox spinner who couldn't believe his luck when he was selected in the Australian squad. With some question marks lingering over Gary Gilmour, who had struggled with gout during the Australian summer, Bright thought he might even make his Test debut in the landmark match. It wasn't to be but he was just glad to be part of the action. He didn't play a Test on Australia's 1977 tour of New Zealand but topped the bowling averages with 25 wickets at 16. He'd first toured the country as a 19-year-old with Ian Chappell's team three years earlier. Bright had been on the periphery of Australian selection ever since but found it hard to break into the side. Twelfth man status for a number of Tests had given Bright a taste of Test cricket but he wanted to savour it for himself.

Bright debuted for Victoria as an 18-year-old against New South Wales at the SCG, taking three wickets with his left-arm orthodox, scoring 67 as a nightwatchman and backing it up with 38 in the second innings.

Bright combined a job in worker's compensation claims for a New Zealand company with a budding cricket career as he found his way through the ranks:

> *I never felt out of place playing Shield cricket. I had always played against men and so the moves up through the grades weren't overly daunting for me. I had also gone to watch Victoria play at the MCG and was steeped in cricket.*

Thirty-two wickets at 19 in his second season for Victoria saw Bright selected for the Australian side to tour New Zealand in 1974, where he was suddenly sharing a dressing room with the likes of Ashley Mallett, Kerry O'Keeffe, the Chappells, Rod Marsh and Doug Walters. The learning curve was steep, although Bright learned how to vary his bowling to different players: 'I learned how to beat the batsman in the air with curve dip and spin and that as a spin bowler what the ball did in the air was very important.'

It was a lesson Bright didn't forget when he played cricket in the Lancashire League in 1975, where he was able to get wickets readily on slow-turning wickets through the use of spin bowling. During the pace-dominated Ashes-winning series of 1974–75, Bright secured only 11 first-class wickets for Victoria. The wickets gradually returned: 4–48 in the second innings in a losing side against South Australia at the MCG in December of 1975 and 4–37 in the second innings against New South Wales in a 146-run win at the MCG a few weeks later. Bright's groove returned when he followed 4–68 against New South Wales at the SCG with 5–36 against the eventual Shield winners, Western Australia, at the

WACA in November of 1976. Bright was elevated to twelfth man status for the third Test against Pakistan and then selection on the Australian tour of New Zealand.

The one who missed out? Alan Turner.

Australia's left-hand opener, Alan Turner, was wondering what he'd done wrong. Sure he hadn't had a great tour of New Zealand, but he wasn't alone. He was looking forward to playing in the Centenary Test and then going on his second tour of England. He received the news from the Australian selectors that he wouldn't be playing in the 100-year celebration of Test cricket: 'We just want to give the selectors a chance to see what this young bloke David Hookes looks like, that's all.' 'Fair enough', Turner thought, 'I'll still be on the plane to England.' But it wasn't to be.

With Hookes' inclusion McCosker moved up to open and Cosier was promoted from the middle order to number three.

Turner had looked a little out of place among the macho cricket culture of the 1970s. Compact and efficient as an opener, he had initially been selected as a stopgap before convincing selectors he had more to offer.

He had in fact come to Test cricket almost as an afterthought, about to retire from Shield cricket in 1975. Jet-black wavy haired with thick eyebrows and sideburns, olive skin and cherub-faced, Turner looked like a choirboy with his impish grin. Always neat-looking on the field, on a risky day he might allow two buttons open on his shirt, sleeves rolled up past the elbow. He looked a bit like a school teacher or a bank teller.

When he batted his happy expression turned solemn, his backside pushed out like he was stopping someone from squeezing by him in a corridor. He dressed neat but batted ugly, just a nudger and a pusher, never a stylist. But he could play. He'd toured South Africa as an Australian schoolboy and New Zealand with a national second 11. By the time he was 24 he thought he'd reached the zenith by playing for New South Wales. Having rung his wife Carolyn to say that he was about to retire and that he would ring his boss and demand a real job, Turner discovered he'd been selected to tour England with the 1975 Australian team and was presented with bottles of champagne along with fellow state Test-touring team-mates Gary Gilmour and Rick McCosker.

Early retirement plans from cricket were put on ice. The first man to score a one-day hundred for Australia, Turner had snuck into the touring side at the expense of Ian Redpath, who stayed at home to keep his antique store afloat.

He marked his Test debut one month short of his 25th birthday. He managed only 68 runs in five innings but was picked for the first Test against the West Indies where he scored 81. His great moment came when he displayed his ability to cut the fast bowlers regularly and with force to score 136 against the West Indies. His next six Tests saw him make only one more half century which led to his dropping, averaging just 29. Three years later, still only 27, he retired from first-class cricket and worked for many years for Benson & Hedges, which was the leading sponsor of Australian cricket for several years. By the time the Centenary Test rolled around, Turner had played fourteen Tests, scored a Test century against the West Indies and a one-day century in the inaugural Cricket World Cup in 1975.

Despite assurances he would be on the plane to England later that year, it was not to be and his time in Australian colours ended almost as suddenly as it had begun.

XI

IAN DAVIS AND GARY COSIER

REMEMBER

IAN DAVIS

Batting always looked easy for 23-year-old Ian Davis. He had an elegance and fluidity in the way he moved to hit the ball. He also had the vital factor that all top-class players have—the time to get into position and play the stroke. Sometimes players like that are criticised when they get out, as the game looks all too easy. It can falsely give the impression you are not trying. England's David Gower as a classic example for someone whom the game looked too easy.

Wiry in build, he was fleet-footed to spinners and an effective opener, leaning more towards playing off the back foot. At times he moved so smoothly it looked like he was gliding towards the ball.

Most cricketers- reach Test playing-status after several hard earned seasons playing for their state, learning the vagaries of the four-day game. It normally means that they will have some time to adjust their game when bowlers begin to work out their technique. Players often experience a case of the second-year blues, where they struggle after some initial success. The skills needed to build the resilience and adaptability to cope with changing demands of a versatile bowling line-up are developed during these seasons. Ian Davis was only 19 years old and had played just five first-class games when he was awarded a baggy green cap. To say he was unprepared was an understatement. When Davis arrived at the MCG to play his first Test he hadn't met five of the players and had only played on the Australian home of cricket once.

Missing from the previous summer's Test against Pakistan was the amiable and popular Ross Edwards. While Davis felt welcomed when he first entered the Australian dressing room, there was a niggling feeling that some felt Edwards should have been playing:

> *I was only 20 and most of the established players were in their late 20s and they had a pretty cliquey group. They were all good about it but I felt they were wondering why Edwards had been dropped.*

On his first day in Test cricket, Davis watched as his team-mates Keith Stackpole (122) Ian Chappell (54) Greg Chappell (60) and Doug Walters (79) piled on the runs. Davis was undefeated on 15 at the end of the day. Davis was dismissed from the first ball he faced the next day, wafting at a gentle outswinger from Richard Hadlee.

He thinks it was just one indication he was not yet ready to make the jump to Test level. Davis believes two or three seasons of playing first-class cricket would have made a big difference to his early performances in Test cricket:

> *That time teaches you to get used to a higher class of cricket. You are going to go through stages where it is quite competitive and you learn a lot over that two to three years before you play for Australia. In hindsight I would have rather that than being thrown in the deep end.*

Davis struggled early in Test cricket, making starts but not much more. He also struggled in his second season of first-class cricket, although he managed 90 against the visiting MCC side.

Greg Chappell lured Davis across the border to Queensland the following summer to open the batting, a position familiar to him at grade level but not first-class. Being young and impressionable and up for change, Davis accepted Chappell's invitation. A transfer with the Commonwealth Bank to the Brisbane office also made the shift a relatively straightforward one. The job originally procured with the help of former Test player Alan Davidson was a handy arrangement. He was given time off with either full-or half-pay.

The most profound incident in Davis' short life was the death of his flatmate and fellow New South Welshman Martin Bedkober whom Davis helped move across the border to play in Queensland. They ended up flatmates and team-mates at Toombul. Davis well remembers the day that Bedkober died.

It was 13 December 1975 at Oxenham Park and Jeff Thomson's and Ian Davis' flat mate was batting for Toombul on a green-top wicket. Bedkober was struck in the chest by a ball from a medium-pace bowler. The 22-year-old batsman stood still for a few seconds waving fieldsmen away, as if to say 'I'm alright', and then collapsed flat on his face (just as Phil Hughes did when he was struck in 2014).

Davis remembers Bedkober gasping for air but thought he was winded and would be okay:

> We got into the ambulance and they called the game off. We were in the waiting room and the doctor asked if there was anyone close to Martin there. He took me behind the curtain and said, Look he's been hit in the heart and unfortunately he's had a haematoma and it's bled and it had caused him to die.

Davis had to ring Bedkober's mother to tell her that her son had died. Davis also had to pack up all of Martin's belongings and take them down to Sydney to give to his parents. It affected Davis and the next time be batted he wore a foam guard on his heart and tied it around his chest.

By 1976–77 Davis was back with New South Wales scoring 106 against Victoria and 158 against South Australia to regain his Test place. A first-innings ton again Pakistan in Adelaide brought up with a pulled six over the Victor

Richardson Gates ensured a selection on Australia's tour of New Zealand.

The two-Test tour of New Zealand proved to be a time for starts but not much else for Davis, with scores of 34, 22, 13 and six not out.

What Davis did notice was the presence of John Cornell who he describes as 'hanging around like a bad smell': 'We were all having drinks and he'd be there. We just thought that given he was Dennis' manager that the tour gave a chance for him to spend some with him.'

By the time of the Centenary Test Ian Davis was a fully-fledged Test cricketer. 'I felt more hardened for Test cricket the second time.'

GARY COSIER

The Centenary Test proved to be a turning point for Australia's Gary Cosier; a division between success and failure. Cricketing life would never be the same for him after this match.

Cosier first played for Victoria as a lanky 18-year-old, opening with Bill Lawry in four innings, all of which were starts, but his highest score was 34. By the time he was 21, and with a couple of average grade seasons behind him, the door to Victorian selection, with the likes Keith Stackpole, Ian Redpath and Paul Sheahan already in the team, appeared closed. Cosier moved to South Australia for the 1974–75 season where, despite not scoring a century, he made 629 runs at 34. Cosier also found he developed enormously by watching Chappell play:

> When I went over to South Australia I was basically an off-side player but after a few months of watching Ian Chappell play on the on side I understood there were two sides to the wicket. Also, the chats we had after play over a beer really helped me understand my own game and the vagaries of cricket overall.

South Australia won the Shield the next season, 1975–76, going from last to first, and Cosier had the time of his life.

Fifth in the national aggregate with 937 runs at 55, Cosier's inaugural first-class ton came in 1975 in South Australia's opening match with 130 against the West Indies. He was rewarded first with a one-day international at his new home ground against the West Indies. Cosier managed to take the wicket of Gordon Greenidge, caught and bowled, and eked out an undefeated 38 as Australian cruised to a five-wicket win.

Cosier's Test debut against the visitors was in the Third Test. He met Jeff Thomson who had recently spent a few hours 'threatening to kill him' in the MCG nets. Max Walker and Ian Chappell also made sure the new boy felt at ease with a few beers on the eve of the Test match. Cosier was used to Ian Chappell's small marks of support that he would get over a few beers after play each day for South Australia.

Cosier, who was more used to a crowd of a few hundred when playing Shield cricket, debuted for Australia in front of 85,661 at the MCG to witness Greg Chappell win the toss and send the West Indies in.

'Like a bolt of lightning' was how he described the pace of the ball that he dropped off West Indies opener Roy Fredericks (who'd just come off a match-winning 169 at Perth) on the first ball of the match. 'I was in the gully and the ball hit the top of my fingers and I thought at least I stopped it going for six!' That was his last mistake of the match. Coming in to bat in the final session of the second day at 4–188, Cosier had to contend with Andy Roberts and the second new ball. Fans may have been puzzled by the Australian captain Greg Chappell seemingly allowing the Test debutant to take most of Robert's bowling; so was Cosier. An old Channel 7 World of Sport interview had Chappell saying, 'No-one should get too excited about the newcomer until he scored runs away from South Australia.' Cosier reflected on the innings, 'I think Greg faced about five balls from Roberts and the new ball until stumps.'

Cosier was still there at stumps and at lunch on day three as well, precariously sitting on 99, all too aware that the last man to make lunch one shy of the milestone had perished on the first ball after lunch. Arthur Chipperfield's debut innings in the first Test at Trent Bridge in 1934 finished one shy of three figures. Cosier played and missed off the first ball after lunch and hit the next ball for four, becoming just the eleventh Australian to hit a ton on debut.

Lillee (4–56) and Thomson's (5–62) first-innings blitz of nine wickets between them, along with Redpath's century (102) and Cosier's (109), helped Australia to an eight-wicket win.

The summer of 1976–77 loomed as unusual in so much as Australia would only play three Test matches against Pakistan before they toured New Zealand for a two-Test series then closed the season with the celebrated Centenary Test

After success against Pakistan including a big hundred (168) at the MCG Cosier had a lukewarm Test series against New Zealand where he'd only managed a couple of starts (23 in Australia's gargantuan total of 552 in the first Test at Christchurch, followed by 23 in the second at Auckland), at just 24 Cosier was seen to be a strong part of the future of Australian Test cricket.

He likens the feel before the Centenary Test match to playing in a footy grand final. For the first time there was a team meeting before the game. A meeting where views about Don Bradman were openly shared. Greg Chappell and Rod Marsh led the meeting:

> *We all went up to the top of the Hilton hotel for a team meeting and chatted about the opposition and then all of a sudden all this vitriol about Bradman spewed out. Bradman got a bigger server than the Poms did.*

Cosier now thinks this was all part of the backdrop with the signings that were taking place:

> *The view was that Bradman was very different as an administrator to what he had been as a player. As a player he sought commercial opportunity but when he was on the Board the senior players thought he tried to nail the players down for as little as he could. There was the perception that the players were bringing the crowds back to the cricket and the Board were reluctant to reward the players more.*

CHAPTER XII

THE LEAD-UP TO THE MATCH

Cricket was everywhere in March 1977. There was even a computer Test to mark the occasion, The News Limited Honeywell 64/20 computer Test, which Australia won in the last quarter-hour of the match. Australia's 345 and 2–241 defeated England 360 and 225. One of the surprises of the computer Test was that Bradman scored only 20 and 44.

More controversially, on the first day of the Centenary Test the headline from Tony Greig's column in *The Australian* was: 'If chant ruins concentration, our batsmen will pull away.'

Greg Chappell wrote back '…and when they do the MCG crowd will rip them to bits.'

Late news was that Bob Woolmer, who had only opened against Australia three times, would open the batting and Amiss would drop down the order. The veteran right-hand batsman, Keith Fletcher, also retained his place at the expense of Graham Barlow and Geoff Miller, who had both played well at Perth.

This was something of a shock and looked like a move to protect Amiss from the pace of Dennis Lillee. Amiss had, after all, averaged 50 opening the batting against India.

On the day of the match a Frank and Ernest Cartoon by Bob Thaves wrote: 'My ambition was to become a legend in my own time, but the best I could make was an unsubstantiated rumour.' A few legends would come out of this match.

It was journalist Murray Hedgecock's first visit to the MCG in 26 years:

*When you come from Victoria your boyhood introduction
to the game was in the grey, echoing cavern of the outer,
standing looking out across the pavilion and stands where
the Melbourne Society and cricket heavyweights were based
then the MCG spells cricket. You know it's Melbourne when
the kids selling the official souvenir booklet wear VFL dust
coats and shout 'Record'.*

THE CURATOR

By Friday 11 March, with the game only a day away, there was a great
deal of interest in the state of the pitch. In his 42-year career, curator Bill
Watt could not recall a Test match being played so late in the year. The
Melbourne strip was slower than most other Test venues across the country.
It was traditionally a seamers' wicket that was prone to life on the first day
but would then even out to become a strong batting wicket. When Watt
prepared the pitch he probably had in the back of his mind the need for a
wicket that would last until the fifth day when the Queen was due to visit.

Watt had the necessary knowledge to perform such a role. Watt was the
son of a Scottish emigrant and Gallipoli veteran who qualified in agriculture
at Sydney Technical College. Bill 'Grassy' Watt, was initially the SCG's
head curator from 1951–58 after joining the SCG staff as an assistant
groundsman in 1935, aged 17. After serving with the RAAF during the
Second World War, Watt returned to the SCG and was appointed assistant
curator to Wally Gorman in 1947. Watt was officially appointed as Head
Curator in April 1951, after the death of Gorman. Watt left Sydney in 1957
to take over as curator at the MCG where he continued the restoration of
the ground after its use during the 1956 Olympics.

Watt was admired by the players for his ability to create pitches that were
fast, grassy and true. Former Australian opening batsman Sidney Barnes
wrote that Watt, 'Could make couch [grass] sprout on grandpa's bald pate.'

Watt was lured to the MCG in 1958 to receive the highest salary ever paid to a curator in Australia and remained head curator for 20 years. So high was Watt's profile that when the former Prime Minister and cricket lover Sir Robert Menzies saw Watt at the MCG he'd say, 'Ah Watt—the fellow we pinched from Sydney.'

Menzies' link with Watt produced some great cricketing folklore. At the end of the 1955 Test against England, Australia had lost the Test match after being bowled out by England speedster, Frank 'Typhoon' Tyson. Watt was standing guard in the middle making sure spectators didn't souvenir parts of the pitch when the Prime Minister walked out to examine the pitch himself. Menzies had seen Australia lose their last eight wickets for 36 runs and apparently was wondering if the pitch was to blame. A close examination of the pitch convinced him that the fault lay with Australia's batsmen and he complimented Watt on producing a fine pitch.

More than two decades later Watt's work would again be closely scrutinised. For what was being spruiked as the most important Test match in the game's one hundred-year history, Watt wanted to get the strip right.

THE QUEEN'S VISIT

The presence of the Queen on the final day of the match was one of the great coups for the organisers of the Centenary Test. Looking back, it's hard to imagine the significance of this for the Australian cricket administrators at the time. We view the monarchy differently to the way it was perceived in Australia in 1977. There was enormous excitement in cricketing circles that the Queen would be present on the final Day of the Centenary Test to watch the action and meet the players at the tea interval. Despite rumblings about an Australian Republic from former Prime Minister Gough Whitlam, Australia was still very much a country with a strong respect for Royalty. These were the days before the royal scandals were made public and any royal visit was greatly anticipated and well attended by the general public.

The Queen was in Australia for a 27-day visit from 7–30 March to mark the year of her silver jubilee and criss-crossed the nation visiting every state, including her first visit to South Australia and Western Australia since 1963.

The Queen was front-page news wherever she went. On 10 March, just two days before the Centenary Test, *The Australian's* front page reported that the Queen had arrived in Queensland in a banana-yellow dress, receiving an effusive welcome from the state's premier Joh Bjelke-Petersen and his wife Flo. While Flo had been practising her curtsies on the tarmac, Joh had been reminding everyone that the Queen was the Queen of Queensland. (In 1973, Joh had tried to get the High Court to recognise the Queen as the Queen of Queensland to prevent Gough Whitlam from declaring Australia a Republic. With the stroke of a pen, Joh ended up doing it a different way by writing the Governor into the Queensland Constitution so there had to be a referendum on the question.)

The night before, the former Prime Minister, Gough Whitlam, had raised some eyebrows at an official reception in Canberra when he said, 'I find the Queen of Queensland sounding somewhat strange. Who's next? The Queen of Siberia?'

The Queen's every official move was reported, even the fact that she was met by a crowd of 8000 at Brisbane's City Hall under raining skies with not a ray of sunshine.

While he may not have been bestowed the honour of an Australian knighthood in 1977, Prince Phillip's actions were also keenly observed. We were told that the Prince was in a buoyant mood as he talked to the crowd and asked a young teenage girl, 'What's written on your T shirt?' The girl, in response, stuck out her chest and showed him, 'Baby, light my fire'. The Prince was reported to have roared with laughter before declining the invitation and moving on.

From there the royal couple travelled on to Launceston in Tasmania and Sydney and Newcastle in New South Wales before arriving in Melbourne.

THE PROGRAM

Those buying the official match program would have noticed a photograph of Dennis Lillee on the cover, appealing for an lbw against England's John Edrich at the MCG. Rod Marsh, Greg Chappell and Doug Walters also join the appeal. A red imprint of the number 100 partly covers and surrounds the shot. It sold for one dollar and featured the Centenary Test logo of a left-handed batsman surrounded by the words Test cricket, England, Centenary and Australia in a rectangular frame, in the top, left corner.

Cricket and advertisements were combined throughout the program. The inside cover had a blurred colour shot of a bowler in delivery stride with the words Wrigley's Chewing Gum. Great Sports'. TAA got into the act as 'the official domestic airline to the Centenary Test' showing a picture of the First English team brought to the colony by Spiers and Pond playing to a packed crowd done up in their finery, complete with a stage coach for some of the spectators. There were even once in a century wine offers with Hardy's Test centenary Riesling, vintage 1976, one of the wines on offer.

Bradman in his article 'Safety Valve for the Space Age: cricket has to be flexible to adapt to the requirements of the times', noted that:

> *The co-operation and understanding between players and officials is extremely good, and where differences are highlighted they usually find their roots in the player who resents that discipline and control which is essential for the general good and conduct of the game, and by that sensationalism which is such an elixir for the media.*

The disconnect between Bradman's comments and the players' wishes gives some idea as to why Kerry Packer found such a willing audience. Bradman, though, could see the value of the one-day game:

> *Today's circumstances demand that with all its shortcomings we must not only settle for a time limit (for Test cricket) but also for a measure of one-day games whereas to win you don't have to dismiss your opponents but only stop them scoring, a theory anathema to many cricket lovers and contrary to the whole purpose and concept of the game.*

Ironically, one of the great drivers of World Series Cricket, Tony Greig, is pictured in an advert for Nutri-Grain. Dressed in his whites, he sits at a breakfast table about to shovel some of the cereal into his mouth: 'If you'd like a real change for breakfast, this is it! Kellogg's Nutri-Grain…a great start if you have to eat and run.'

A new device for communications, the remote control, was advertised with a Phillips Natural Colour TV 'with a digital read out so you can tell at a glance what channel you are watching'.

All 235 players and umpires invited to the Centenary Test were listed, including New South Wales' Jack Moroney, whose only Test appearance against Bill Brown's English side in 1950–51 resulted in a pair of ducks.

XIII

CHAPTER

MATCH DAY

So significant was the hype surrounding the match it led Rod Marsh to declare, 'I thought that there was no way the game could live up to all the hype.'

On match day the Australian public woke up to a special edition of *The Australian* newspaper with a special wrap around announcing 'Match of the Century'.

A colour, souvenir issue to commemorate a century of Tests between England and Australia featured team photos of the Australian side to New Zealand and England's tour of India. With the photos having been taken weeks before the match, the most spoken-about player, David Hookes, having not toured New Zealand, wasn't even featured.

An action shot of DK Lillee, a young Don Bradman and WG Grace, looking seriously at the camera, were featured as was a photo of England captain Tony Greig, shown pulling a ball to mid-wicket. The punters who paid their 15 cents for this edition with the special Centenary Test logo on the upper-right corner were also greeted with some historical statistics to consider. This was to be the 225th encounter between the sides, but there were no Ashes at stake (Australia still held them after destroying England 4–1 and then defeating England at home 1–0). Australia, the home side, had won 87 Tests to England's 71 while 66 were drawn. Of the 119 Tests played in Australia, the home side won 59 to England's 43 with 17 drawn. Of those played in England, both sides had recorded 28 wins with 49 matches drawn.

Thanks to Benson & Hedges' sponsorship, the winning side would be taking home $9000 while the loser would receive $4500 and the man of the match would attract $1500. The VCA presented a commemorative medallion to each member of the teams, a replica of the original medallion presented to the Australian and England sides

THE HYPE SURROUNDING THE MATCH

There was great hype surrounding the match, although the Queen's speech before Parliament in Canberra on Thursday 10 March managed to move the Test coverage to one side of the front pages. John Monks, a royal correspondent, wrote, 'instead of the usual Royal Orstralia that has grated in the Strine ears for years she said Australia or Australian time and again without the slightest hesitation.'

Leading up to the Centenary Test the Australians, returning from a brief two-Test tour of New Zealand, had little idea of the build-up to the match. Test captain Greg Chappell thought it 'just another match no bigger or smaller than any other.' That was until he arrived at Melbourne airport and saw an array of past Australian and England greats walking by. Greeted by the ABC's Norman May with microphone, he looks surprised after being accosted. 'When we started to arrive at the MCG and all the past name plates were up on the Members stand we started to realise the importance, gravity and history of the match.'

The match itself was squeezed in to the tail end of a summer that saw Pakistan tour for a three Test series, a tour of New Zealand and then, following the Centenary Test, a tour of England.

Chappell remembers the Australians working hard on their fitness and fielding on the trans-Tasman tour, knowing the challenges that lay ahead.

It was only when he arrived in Melbourne that Greg Chappell started to contemplate the historical significance of playing in a Test match to celebrate the first ever Test (his grandfather Vic Richardson had captained Australia).

Chappell thought his side had the right to be considered slight favourites because of the advantage of playing on an Australian wicket. He wrote in his column in *The Australian:*

> *There will be a lot of tension and pressure on both sides*
> *but if we apply the same approach and attitude that we*
> *did in New Zealand we will do well. We have had a good*
> *preparation and by the end of the New Zealand tour Dennis*
> *Lillee was jumping out of his skin.*

How prophetic those words proved to be.

The significance of the match was highlighted when Greg Chappell was handed a specially minted gold medallion as he walked out to the middle of the MCG with Tony Greig. So elaborate was the coin that the captains had to have the coin explained to them to ensure they understood which side was the heads and which was tails. For the first time, the captains were accompanied by a throng of media and photographers, something that would become commonplace in the modern game.

Rick McCosker had also noted a sense of excitement on the first morning of the match:

> *The first day was so tense, there was excitement everywhere*
> *and noise everywhere and it was the biggest crowd that I*
> *had played in front of. Everyone was tense and nervous.*
> *Everyone was just so excited to be a part of this event.*

By 10am nearly 60,000 spectators were in the ground. An opening ceremony ensued with a massed services band entertaining the crowd before the chairman of the ACB, Bob Parish, led the two teams, and an impressive list of former England and Australian captains, to the ground where they fanned out in a semicircles facing the outer of the grounds, a modern player alternated with a former great. The oldest captain present was the 87-year-old Jack Ryder, who led Australia in the 1928–29 series (sadly he would die two weeks after the Centenary Test). The most senior English captain was Bob Wyatt, the home skipper in the 1934 rubber and living witness to Bradman's score of 304 at Leeds that year.

There they were, a cavalcade of players…heroes to young fans who had long ago grown to adulthood. Introduced in succession by Parish were 'Gubby' Allen, Don Bradman, Norman Yardley, Lindsay Hassett, Freddie Brown, Ian Johnson, Len Hutton, Richie Benaud, Peter May, Bobby Simpson, Ted Dexter, Bill Lawry, Colin Cowdrey, Mike Smith, Mike Denness, Tony Greig and Ian and Greg Chappell.

Bill Lawry recalled feeling humbled by the experience:

> *Many (of the other captains) had been childhood heroes, others were team-mates of undoubted calibre or legendary English skippers with whom I'd had some intense battles. I floated off the ground with a lump in my throat and a tear in my eye.*

The former players left the field to a roaring cheer, giving the impression to those approaching the ground at the last minute that the game had already begun and that there was an early wicket.

It was a time for high emotion for past and present players. Greg Chappell was interviewed by the ABC's Norman May on arriving in Adelaide from Brisbane, who said, 'You qualify as both a current and a former player.' Chappell responded, 'I feel more like a former player at the moment.' It was understandable that he may have felt a little jaded. It had been a hectic summer already.

Ian Chappell stood out in the captains parade. Rather than wear the traditional Melbourne Cricket Club dress code of a suit and tie, Ian Chappell had dressed in a green safari suit. It was yet another statement to cricket authorities that he wasn't going to toe the line. In retrospect, it also appears to have been an up yours to the cricketing establishment and a hint of what was to come. By then he had retired from Test and state cricket and was playing district cricket for North Melbourne. If Chappell had been rebellious when he played for his state and country, he certainly wasn't going to conform to the wishes of authority now.

THE GREAT CONTRAST

The Melbourne Cricket Club also hosted four lavish official functions around the Centenary Test. Each event hosted up to 600 people. As well as these functions there were numerous cocktail parties and other celebratory events, such as the appearance of a big band and the Centenary mile race during the lunch break on Monday, involving Olympic Gold medallist, New Zealander John Walker.

The range of souvenirs created for the match by the ACB was unprecedented. 'You wouldn't get a better range at Disneyland or outside a Bangkok temple', Keith Dunstan said. It appeared that no expense was spared. Mike Bingham in the Melbourne *Sun* also observed, 'other cricket matches have been telecast and sponsored but no game has been so superbly marketed.'

The Australian Cricket Board in combination with the Franklin Mint Pty ltd, a handsome collectors' wallet called the Test Cricket Centenary Official Commemorative 1877–1977; a limited edition combining a solid sterling silver medal with five Australian post stamps and officially post marked at the site of the first Test on the exact Centenary date, 15 March 1977.

More than two hundred officials, groundsmen contracted labourers rushed to have everything ready for the big match. Painters were working overtime to make sure the MCG had a special glean. Outside the ground in the car park a mini post office was open,

As Christopher Forsyth observed in his book *Pitched Battles,* Australia Post:

> *...hired a beautiful girl wearing clothes straight out of Thomas Hardy, to sell first day covers. Miss Philately they called her and they put her in a log cabin at the MCG that looked more like a Kentucky Fried Chicken Coop than a post office.*

A $6484 Toyota Celica lift back sedan was the prize on offer for a mark the ball competition, called the Centenary Test sun ball, with the $1 a shot proceeds going to the Lord Mayor's bushfire appeal fund.

Flags were atop the Northern stand…Benson & Hedges, the cigarette company driven out of TV advertising were still getting in on the act with huge circling signs behind the bowler at the southern end. The flags of Qantas, the airline that flew the English VIPs from London, and TAA the official carrier of Australian VIPs and Greig's men from Perth were also featured at the ground. Signs of money and sponsorship were everywhere.

The attention to detail was extraordinary. When former England batsman Eddie Paynter couldn't adjust his palate to the cold Australian beer during the lunch break on Monday, VCA stewards warmed his beer under a tap. On the same subject, the bar manager reported a roaring trade with 16 barrels of beer consumed each day of the match. 'It was like having five football grand finals in one week' reported Pat Kelly, the bar manager.

Inside the large marquee erected over the outdoor practice wicket, workers were rushing to complete a bar which would have three closed-circuit colour TVs for patrons to watch the game. The indoor cricket area was spruced up to accommodate a dining area for the 218 past players, umpires and officials.

Inside and outside the ground teams from TV stations were busy setting up equipment. The ABC had Keith Miller, Paul Sheahan, Frank Tyson and Norman May in its commentary team while the 10 network had Richie Benaud, Bill Lawry, Ian Chappell, Bob Simpson and Geoff Boycott, in a curious mix of the forces that would help define the cricket war between the establishment and Kerry Packer's World Series cricket over the next two years.

After the national anthem the chairman of the Australian Cricket Board, Bob Parish, declared the game on and handed the specially minted gold medallion to the Australian captain to toss. 'This will certainly be a Test to remember and just as certainly a Test of memories.'

Footage showed Greg Chappell and Tony Greig walking to the middle, blanketed on either side with cameramen, with the Australian captain pointing out what was on the coin and turning it over to show each side.

Chappell can't remember what was on the coin but can remember the presence of media:

> We used to just go out into the middle and toss the coin, there might be a photographer there for the first Test of the series but normally there wasn't. This time there were cameramen and other officials surrounding us. It was the first time I had seen such a fuss at the toss. It was perhaps a sign as to what would later follow.

In the autumnal coolness of a south-westerly breeze, the two skippers approached the well-grassed wicket with the coin glinting as it spun high in the air—the game was on in earnest.

THE FINAL MCC LINE-UP

Tony Greig called correctly and sent Australia in to bat, indicative that Greig wanted to protect his batsmen from the pace of Dennis Lillee. Greig knew that the MCG wicket was at its liveliest on the first morning. England opener Dennis Amiss had been dropped down the order to number four to protect him from Lillee, who had removed him eight times in the previous ten innings.

Amiss knew the Melbourne wicket well. He'd scored 90 in an innings in the Third Test in 1974–75, the one and only time he had appeared confident in the series. Amiss admitted to 'a certain nervousness about playing but I was confident about playing in Melbourne where I knew it was a seamers' wicket.'

Many Australian cricket fans, having witnessed Amiss' destruction at the hands of Dennis Lillee in 1974–75, wondered at the logic behind the decision to play Amiss. In the England batsman's defence, Amiss had scored 203 against an attack containing Andy Roberts, Wayne Daniel, Michael Holding and Vanburn Holder, a series Australian had only heard about in fleeting news reports or brief newspaper articles. These were the times before the 24-hour news cycle and live coverage of foreign matches on pay television. Amiss' opening spot went to Kent all-rounder Bob Woolmer who had opened only three times against Australia in Tests for England but had scored 149 at the Oval to thwart the Aussies' winning efforts.

Veteran right-hand batsman Keith Fletcher retained his place at the expense of Graham Barlow, a promising young batsman and outstanding fieldsman. Geoff Miller, who along with Barlow, had done well in the match against Western Australia, also missed out. In the bowling department Derek Underwood remembers it being a close call and that 'hours were spent deliberating over whether Randall or Barlow would be picked in the side'.

England also had their new bowling hero, John Lever, who had made headlines with 26- wickets at just 14 a piece during a gruelling Indian tour. Lever represented an unknown quantity to the Australians, and being a left-arm seamer who slanted the ball across the batsman, a less familiar opponent.

DAY ONE OF THE CENTENARY TEST

As the players completed their pre-match nets session Gary Cosier wondered who might bat at number three for Australia. He had batted at numbers five or six in New Zealand and got starts but was not in the type of form to be promoted to number three. 'There was no Turner so I assumed that I would bat at number four and that Greg Chappell would bat at first drop.'

Cosier would be told the morning of the match that Rick McCosker, who had been batting at number three in New Zealand, was to open the batting with Ian Davis and he would bat at three. The move seems an odd one. Just the season before, Test debutant Graham Yallop was asked to bat at number three against the West Indies when he had been batting in the middle order for Victoria. It was well known that Greg Chappell preferred to bat at number four so maybe there was little choice.

Tony Greig won the toss and elected to bowl. Greg Chappell had already decided to bat so the result of the toss itself was inconsequential.

No doubt caught up in the excitement of the match and then the nervous tension associated with watching the pre-match festivities, the English side ran onto the MCG with as much life as a football team before a grand final. This was quite different to what we would normally see at a Test match where players would traditionally walk onto the field with the occasional player breaking into a light jog. All this added to the feel of the game being more like a football final than a cricket match.

Greg Chappell noted that, 'the wicket boasted a little moisture and I had no doubt it would provide the bowlers with normal first session assistance, but I didn't think that it posed too many problems.'

The weather was overcast with a strong south-west breeze coming down the ground when England's opening bowler, John Lever, off a 22-pace run, bowled the first ball to opener Ian Davis. As if directly opposing the hype and ceremony we had just witnessed, the ball harmlessly passed wide of off stump, giving the Australian opener an early sight of the new ball. The early impressions were that there wasn't much menace in the wicket. Greig had placed a field that was a combination of attack and defence, as if almost uncertain as to how to proceed; wanting to attack, as he had sent Australia in, but not wanting to give many runs away.

The field consisted of three slips, a gully, deep backward point, cover, mid-on, leg slip and fine leg. Not that there was much for the fielders to do in Levers first two wayward overs. An ironic cheer went up when Davis played the fifth delivery—the first time Lever had been on target.

McCosker tried to hook Willis' first delivery and, in an omen for what was to come, was struck on the wrist. The crowd was eerily quiet as if unsure what to make of this celebratory occasion.

The first run of the innings was a leg bye off McCosker's pads. Davis ducked a Willis bouncer and then hit the ball past mid-on for two runs, the first off the bat.

When the score had reached 11 Davis played back to a John Lever in-swinger and was given out lbw by umpire Tom Brooks. To this day, Davis is disappointed with the decision. 'I thought I was a bit unlucky I thought the ball pitched outside leg stump.'

Enter Gary Cosier, whose Test record at the MCG was an impressive two Test matches for two hundreds. Cosier felt confident. 'I thought the MCG was mine and that I could do whatever I wanted there.'

On the surface, life appeared pretty good for Cosier coming back to his home city of Melbourne. Here he was on the biggest sporting stage in the world and he had a good job with a radio station back in Adelaide. Unbeknown to his team-mates Cosier's wife had left him the week before.

'It'll be okay,' he thought, 'I just need to put it out of my mind and concentrate on what's happening in the centre.' While Cosier doesn't remember feeling distracted, recent domestic events much have sat in the recesses of his mind.

Cosier clipped Lever's first ball off his legs, past mid-off, getting off the mark. The next ball perhaps revealed more about Cosier's state of mind when he swished at a ball outside off stump.

The atmosphere was more aggressive than normal; Willis bowling quicker than he had when in Australian two years before, John Lever angling the ball across the right-handers' bodies. The ball was seaming around and the MCG wicket had more bounce than normal. If the Australians could just get through these opening overs they would have a platform to build a decent score upon. The pressure was building.

It began with a small, stuttering step. Bob Willis, England's lanky fast bowler, with his mop of curly hair, charged in. Moving like some rampaging bull down a hill, Willis was stiff-armed with a wild look in his eye. It all happened in a blur. The ball was dropped short, bouncing toward his face. Could it have been lost for a moment in the sea of colour of the crowd just above the sight screen? Australian opening batsman Rick McCosker can't remember. He does remember the sickening thud that came next when five ounces of leather struck his head and, after he was struck, dropping his bat onto his wicket.

His face felt numb rather than pained, although he bled sufficiently to leave a crimson stain on the crease line.

Willis' bouncer was onto McCosker too quickly and the ball struck him on his right jaw, the ball dropped from there on to his right glove before hitting the stumps. The Australian opening batsman dropped his bat and brought both hands to his face before dropping to his knees. Cosier was at the other end. 'There was a dull thud, a deep sickening bang which was usually the worst. I rushed up to him and straight away you knew he was in trouble.'

The morning had been full of distractions. First the pageantry of the pre-match ceremony and then the extra pressure of having to play before all of those greats who were watching on from the Members stand. Overcast conditions had made it harder to pick the ball up in the opening overs. The England team under Tony Greig were aggressive with plenty of sledging early on. They had learnt well from the Australians. That day, though, the gamesmanship had an extra edge to it.

Ray Bright remembered the injury happening just as the players were getting comfortable in their seats. Denis Amiss was standing in the slips when McCosker was hit, 'It was a really nasty crack we could hear straight away that something must have broken.'

Umpire Max O'Connell was at square leg and waved to the grandstand as soon as he arrived at the stricken batsman. It was Dr Graham Beard who came out from the Members area. 'The normal match day doctor had been called to attend to one of the crowd members who had had a heart attack and so out came Doc Beard.'

As McCosker walked off, escorted by Dr Beard, he could only think of the disappointment and the sense of having let his team-mates down. The sight of a crumpling McCosker and Cosier rushing to help his injured team-mate, provides an arresting image of the match. McCosker remembered:

> *It took a while for me to settle down and settle in. In the back of my mind I knew that there were a lot of former players in the stand and you were wondering what they were all thinking, things along the lines of 'these young pups these days are not in the same class as we were'. They probably weren't saying that but that was all part of your imagination and thinking. I really wanted to do well in front of these guys this all adds to the pressure of what was already a big first day…it was pretty daunting. And I think it had a fair bit to do with how we batted on that first day when the conditions favoured the bowling.*

The crowd at last lit up, voicing boisterous concerns from the outer. Australia was 2–13. Greg Chappell was immediately off the mark with a single before Cosier slashed one over the slips for the first boundary of Australia's innings.

When Willis bowled two more bouncers to Greg Chappell the booing grew even louder. For the rest of the match Willis was the target of the Melbourne outer.

Murray Hedgecock wrote of his displeasure at this element of the crowd. 'You don't know whether to laugh or cry or curse when that lunatic note creeps into cricket barracking.'

Cosier, with his short but powerful back-lift, repeated the dose, square cutting past Amiss in the gully. The signs looked good for the ginger-haired Australian. How quickly cricket can change.

Having seen off a slower Lever bouncer that ambled over his left shoulder as he ducked, Cosier tried to hook the next one. The sliding bouncer was on him before he knew it. Cosier followed through with the stroke but the end result looked bad, as the ball spooned to leg gully. Australia was 3–23.

Walking back to the pavilion, crestfallen, the moment seemed a long way from his century on debut against the West Indies, followed up with 168 against the visiting Pakistan side that summer. As Cosier walked off the MCG he thought, 'Well I'll never do that again.'

Bill O'Reilly had watched aghast as 'the hapless Cosier tried to establish a new method of hooking a shortish ball'. Cosier had more swivelled than moved back and across, as a batsman should when playing an adventurous stroke with apparently little regard for his own safety.

The arrival of 21-year-old Davis Hookes attracted great interest. His first run came with a turn to leg from the third delivery he faced from Willis. He was soon driving Lever for three then gliding the Essex left-armer wide of slip for a boundary By the time Hookes cover drove Lever for a boundary he had taken 13 runs off the over.

Forty-one runs were scored in the first hour for the cost of three wickets. Remarkably, with the very long run-ins of Bob Willis and Peter Lever, only nine overs had been bowled. In any circumstances to have bowled so few overs was poor, to have done so on the first day in the biggest Test in one hundred years was indefensible.

Hookes tried another attacking stroke when he tried to pull Lever, with the ball ending up at mid-on. Chris Old, who had just been brought into the attack, removed Hookes with a ball that lifted. Greig, at second slip, gleefully took the chance. Hookes, who had played so fluently, was out to a nasty delivery that rose from just short of a length, which he fended off with a hunched over stroke where he was up on his toes.

Australia's 4–45 quickly became 5–51 when Walters, on four, skied a wild pull at Willis to provide Greig with his second catch of the match.

Walters, so often the hero in such situations by playing his natural game, had greatly misjudged the pace of Willis. Australia added only 26 runs in the second hour to lunch as Chappell and Marsh tried to come to terms with the situation.

Greg Chappell was uncharacteristically playing the sheet anchor role, seemingly insistent on all-out defence.

The break must have done Marsh some good; two back-foot drives past Chris Old saw the Australian wicketkeeper briefly return to the swashbuckler of old. Underwood came into the attack at 5–92 but it was Old who removed Marsh, who tried to give himself room on the back foot and inside edged to Knott. Marsh's opposite number, who had been naturally moving to his left, had to dive to his right to take a spectacular one-handed catch.

Gilmour meekly surrendered to Old for four, hanging his bat out to dry. O'Keeffe then fell to a spectacular catch by Brearley at slip off Underwood; a ball that appeared even quicker through the air than the left-armer's usual delivery and one that bounced more than expected.

At tea Australia was 8–126. Greg Chappell had scored 39 in 204 minutes. Chappell had struggled to exert his usual dominance on the game. He was occasionally able to drive the ball through the packed off-side field but more often had to rely on some deft cutting. He added just one run in 33 minutes before tea. After the break the persistence of Underwood proved too much and Chappell tried an uncharacteristic swipe and was bowled by Underwood, who was greeted enthusiastically by his team-mates for not only dismissing the Australian captain but also reaching the milestone of 250 Test wickets.

Home-town hero Max Walker received a strong cheer from the crowd as he entered the MCG swinging his arms in a circle as if he was preparing to open the bowling rather than going out to bat. The preparation did little; he was out for two. Australia was all out for 138 in 289 minutes off 43.6 overs. It was a matter of poor batting against tight bowling and, most importantly, very good catching. Derek Underwood had mopped up the Australian tail taking 3–16 off 11 overs while the wickets were spread evenly among the England attack notably Lever (2–36), Willis (2–33) and Old (3–39).

England began its innings with a little more than an hour to bat. Lillee opened the bowling to cries of 'Lillee!-Lillee!' from the crowd, making them even more excited when his seventh ball hit Woolmer's shoulder and flew to Greg Chappell at first slip.

The partnership of Bob Woolmer and Mike Brearley, both playing in their first Test in Australia, lasted for 19 runs and 44 minutes before the former fell to Lillee. The last ball of Lillee's fourth over was almost a half volley and Woolmer squeezed it to Chappell at first slip, who held the ball close to the ground.

Derek Underwood was given the unenviable job of being nightwatchman. When the shadows came across the wicket as the sun slid behind the MCG stands the umpires called off play with three minutes remaining.

Tony Greig was interviewed at the end of the day's play and would utter the words, 'This has been one of the great days of Test cricket. If I live to be ninety-five, I'll never forget it.'

The mention of the number 95 proved to be prophetic.

Australia 138 England 1–29 (Brearley 12, Underwood 5) Attendance 61,316

DAY ONE REFLECTIONS

The first mistake made was when an exuberant Melbourne Cricket Club secretary, Ian Johnson, tipped a record-breaking crowd of 100,000 for the opening day. That only 61,316 turned up was disappointing. It reminded Johnson of the old adage of never counting the gate before it's unlatched. People were probably put off with the idea of being squashed in like sardines for the duration of a six-hour day. Johnson took some pleasure knowing that the television audience from 4pm to stumps reached a peak audience in Melbourne and Sydney of 596,000 people according to ratings made available GTV9 Melbourne.

Derek Underwood was surprised by the intensity of the match. 'I thought it was going to be an exhibition match but obviously it was more than that.'

Underwood experienced the first day as both a bowler and a batsman, coming in as nightwatchman facing Lillee's controlled aggression and a hollering Bay 13. Bowling to Greg Chappell, Underwood remembers some 'hold in the wicket' that restricted Chappell's off-side play. Underwood also reflected on how it was only after Greg Chappell played more one-day cricket that he developed better off-side play against him. Remembering the advice of his Kent coach Claude Lewis, 'whatever pitch to bowl on there is a pace to bowl', Underwood held back his usual medium-paced left-arm spinners just a fraction.

After Australia was bowled out for 138 on the first day Jim Laker, the man who took 19 Australian wickets in one Test, wrote, 'What a shocking lot of batsmen. How low has Australia sunk? I cannot recall seeing the Australian batting line up so short of class.'

Chappell responded in his column that, 'this Centenary Test was one of the hardest matches I have played in with unbelievable pressure applied from both sides from the start.'

Bill O'Reilly had little time for the efforts of the Australian side. 'Australia batted…as though the original XI from 1877 had been specially resurrected for this historic job.'

David Hookes remembered that his first innings in Test cricket could easily have ended first ball but for it being a no ball. Hookes' tentative steps back and across to Bob Willis found him caught in front of the wicket. Hookes made 17 displaying some impressive attacking strokes. The problem was not so much that he missed out after getting a start but had more to do with his footwear:

I had batted wearing the same pair of Adidas squash

shoes I had worn while scoring the centuries for South Australia the previous month and, because it was so hot then, my feet had sweated profusely and stained the shoes a dirty colour, son the trademark three white stripes were especially prominent. While I was taking my pads off and feeling miserable about my dismissal David Richards came into the dressing room and said: 'You'll have to change your shoes. You can't wear those again son.

Hookes was right to wonder whether Richards approach was poorly timed but it was typical of the way the Board treated its players. Richards should have known that the worst time to approach a batsman is when he had first been dismissed and to have done so when Hookes had just played his first Test innings in front of more than 61,000 people. Hookes was not only dealing with the disappointment of being dismissed but also the adrenaline rush that comes with performing before such a big crowd with so much at stake. If a message needed to have been passed on to Hookes it could surely have been done with a quiet word in his ear at the end of the day. The colour of a batsman's shoes was hardly a matter of priority. Hookes later wrote:

I realised I should have cleaned the shoes before the match, but they had been lucky for me and I was reluctant to tamper with them in any way before my First Test. I wore the same rubber soled shoes in the second innings, but only after I had whitened them to the stripes weren't anywhere near as noticeable.

Greg Chappell made a laboured three-hour forty, an innings he described as one of the best of his Test career given the pressures that were on the players:

*It's hard to rate innings but in the context of the game and the
conditions I've always rated that as one of my best innings.
Underwood especially was hard to get away. He was
accurate and gripping and holding up. You had to wait and
wait and wait. Unless he gave you room it was hard to score.*

With wickets falling around him Greg Chappell, one of the most
gloriously classical Australian batsmen of all time, had struggled for one
of the few times in his life to break into his usual fluent style of stroke play.
At the time, the Australians wouldn't have known it but Chappell's first
innings score of 40, the top score in the Australian side was crucial to the
end result of a match in which Australia won by just 45 runs:

*We were concerned about survival more than anything else.
It was a very green wicket ideal to bowl on and hard to bat
on....It was the most drained I'd ever felt after batting...
my whole being centred on trying to get a score that would
keep us in the game.*

By the time Australia had been bowled out for 138 Chappell thought
they had done a reasonable job but he wasn't confident they had done
enough for a first innings lead.

When Rick McCosker was struck on the head and bowled by a Bob
Willis bouncer, the Australian captain Greg Chappell was his replacement.

McCosker meanwhile had settled inside the dressing room thinking if he
just laid down on the rubbing table for a while everything would be okay.
Then after a while his whole face started to swell up and there was a huge
amount of blood inside and there was a large lump. The initial inspection
from the doctor concluded that the jaw was just very badly bruised

In a far cry from what would happen today, McCosker lay on the table
for close to two hours. When the bruising around his cheek became bigger
and blacker an orthodontist called for an X-ray. Once in hospital, and while
keeping an ear on the radio from his hospital bed, McCosker was told by the

specialist that he had in fact had his jaw broken in two places. That night the specialists took a plaster impression of the upper and lower jaws and designed a splint that would fit the impression on the upper and lower jaw. His head was also wrapped in bandages with the aim being to keep the jaw immobile.

The next day his wife and two boys were flown down from Sydney as part of a pre-arranged trip (the ACB had rung McCosker's wife to explain the injury and offered to fly them down). While McCosker sat in hospital that night, he took in the news of his injury, finding out afterwards that the break in the jaw had cut across two nerves. He later reflected:

> *My memories of being hit are fairly clear. In hindsight I thought that there's a golden rule when you're playing a Test match at the MCG—never play a cross bat shot in the first session because of the moisture in the wicket and the bounce being a little unpredictable...so I broke the rule and paid the penalty. I should have never tried to play the hook shot in the first hour of a Test match. That was the first thing that went wrong, the second was that the ball hit me and the third was that it landed on my stumps.*

Initially, after being struck, McCosker felt little pain although when he was struck he heard a loud noise in his head:

> *I remember walking off the field and not feeling anything at all. Our physio and then Don Beard came out and as I walked off I thought it wasn't too much of a problem...I heard the English fieldsmen go up because the ball landed on the stumps and dislodged the bails so they didn't register initially that it hit me in the jaw. I remember walking off the field and not feeling anything at all. When I returned to the dressing room there was a bit of blood but there wasn't too much concern apart from the fact that I was out!*

Former England captain Ted Dexter wrote that 'the harsh murmur of resentment' that filled the ground revived memories of the Larwood–Oldfield Bodyline incident of 1932–33.

Bright remembers how surprised they were that McCosker had been hit:

> *Back then there weren't any helmets and we were taught at an early age to watch the ball and get your head out of the way. It was very unusual for someone to get hit especially a top order batsman. When he got to the dressing room we could see the claret and knew he wasn't in a very good way. The injury itself didn't alter the mood of the dressing room much but it was a surprise to see someone hit.*

Bright makes a pertinent point that demonstrates some of the differences between batsmen in the 1970s and now. The modern day batsman, with the benefits of helmets, have traditionally had less fear of being hit and often move to hook off the front foot. Without such a fear it has been less important to track the ball all the way in its path. Players have become more adventurous and perhaps complacent when hooking or pulling the short ball, especially so in the shorter forms of the game such as Twenty20, when a more flamboyant approach to batting is required. A hit in the helmeted head might have been an occupational hazard but one that could be dismissed relatively easily. That was, until the tragic death of Philip Hughes after being struck by a ball in a Shield match while wearing a helmet. We will have to wait to see how batsmen react but the initial signs are, after a brief period of mourning and more care when batting, it is back to business as usual. Some batsmen do, however, now wear helmets with additional padding around the neck.

Australia's opening batsman, Ian Davis, sees it differently. 'I remember plenty of blokes getting struck in the head.' Davis had also seen his friend and flatmate Martin Bedkober killed after being struck by a ball in the chest during a grade game.

Gary Cosier was shattered after the first day's play. On this, the biggest day of his career and having been elevated to the number three, he was out in an embarrassing manner caught hooking for just ten:

> *The ball was right over middle and leg and I just mis-hooked. When I walked off the ground I thought, 'that is the last time I'm ever going to do that'. After he had a shower he walked over and spoke to his schoolboy coach George Murray who was the coach of the University High School for some reassurance.*

At the end of the first day's play England's players gathered at the bar of the Hilton hotel for a few beers. Dennis Lillee remembers seeing most of the England side with smiles across their faces. The mood among the English side would be vastly different the following night.

The question was, had the Australians wilted under the enormous pressure of the occasion or was it a matter of the England side bowling and catching very well in conditions that favoured bowling? The England side was clearly not overawed when they bowled and seemed to relish playing in the heightened atmosphere.

After the first day's play umpires O'Connell and Brooks were called to a meeting with VCA secretary David Richards to talk about the contingency plan should the match finish early. A one-day match to cater for a vacant Thursday and the Queen's visit was discussed. With McCosker injured, Alan Turner was already at the MCG if required.

Doug Walters thought the Test match had almost been ruined because of a poor wicket. 'They tried hard to ruin a sensational Test match because of the wicket…it could have been all over in two days.'

That night, after TAA reception when Australian great Keith Miller tried to head off early he was accosted at the door by television interviewer Roger Climpson who handed him an ornately inscribed journal and led him to a nearby auditorium before stating, 'Keith Miller, at this moment you are on national television and This is Your Life.'

Bill Edrich, Dennis Compton, Ray Lindwall and others crowded into the room for a half hour of memories of air force and post- war cricket days. As former fast bowler and author Frank Tyson noted, 'The Centenary Test social scene was like that; there was no escape.'

CHAPTER

XV

DAY TWO

Despite the great expectations from England that they would mount a large total and effectively bat Australia out of the match, it took Dennis Lillee, from his 33-yard run, just six deliveries to dismiss the opener Mike Brearley. The ball exploded off the pitch, a vicious, lifting outswinger. The scene was set for Brearley, a plodding batsman, to set a strong foundation upon which England could mount a large total, but his luck wasn't in. Brearley fended at a short, rising ball sending it chest high to an ever-grateful David Hookes, taking his first catch in Test cricket.

Batting at number four, the all fidgeting, all talking, Derek Randall attracted attention when, after playing and missing at a rising Lillee delivery, he proceeded to spring to attention and doff his cap, Charlie Chaplin-style, at the fast bowler. 'No good hitting me there mate, nothing to damage,' stated Randall to an incredulous Lillee.

Randall, in his naivety, had just added to Lillee and his fellow Australians' strong drive to bowl England out. Keeper Rod Marsh was quick to inform Randall that this match was 'not a fucking garden party'.

Max Walker's first over of the morning saw him dismiss Underwood, caught by Greg Chappell at slip who juggled a difficult chance. England had slumped to 3–34. Walker returned to fine leg to rapturous applause.

Enter Dennis Amiss to face his nemesis, Lillee. Rarely can a top-order batsman have felt as hesitant as Amiss, who had been dismissed by Lillee nine times in his last 11 innings. Both Amiss, Lillee and the crowd knew that Amiss had been dropped down the order to avoid this very situation, an encounter with Lillee and the new ball.

It's hard to imagine what it must have been like for Amiss standing in the middle of the MCG, where he knew there was huge support for Lillee including signs strewn across the grandstands such as 'We Luv Ya Dennis', all this in addition to the large crowd chanting Lillee's name. Lillee soon had Amiss reeling backwards and almost falling to the ground to try and evade a bouncer. A 180-degree pivot had caused him to lose his cap.

For 18 balls Amiss did his best to survive; a square drive off Lillee for three boosted his confidence but it was all over quickly for Amiss; this time not at the hands of Lillee but rather Walker, when he sparred one to O'Keeffe in the gully, leaving England at 4–40.

Lillee sent down two savage deliveries at Randall, the second one was almost unplayable. The MCG roar matched the Australian side's delight. Randall was soon out, caught behind off Lillee. The upstart had got his comeuppance. With England sitting precariously at 5–40 Tony Greig appeared, swinging his arms around in a windmill-type action as he strode on to the MCG, more like a boxer entering a heavyweight-title bout than an English captain walking out to bat.

Tony Greig and Keith Fletcher added 21 in 26 minutes. An hour had passed and England had lost four wickets for 24. While Greig drove with confidence at Lillee and Walker, Fletcher held on defensively, like a desperate man clutching at the remaining soil of a collapsing cliff. Greig scored 18 in 20 balls before committing one drive too many off Walker, on a ball that moved back late, and England had collapsed to 6–61. The ball had clipped Greig's back pad and was deflected into the middle and leg stumps. Commentating on the ABC former Australian batsman Paul Sheahan described the ball as 'one of the best inswingers I'd ever seen.'

Rarely can an Australian skipper have felt he could attack with every delivery while defending a total of 138.

Gary Gilmour's first ball to Fletcher sailed over the batsman's head, bouncing in front of Marsh, the second was short and very wide of leg stump and the third a no ball. Gilmour was removed from the attack after just five overs and would play only a minor role with the ball in the second innings. This was a huge blow for Australia. Only two years earlier Gilmour helped blitz the England batting line up taking 6–14 in a World Cup semi final at Leeds.

Walker continued to bowl well, dispatching the hapless Fletcher who pushed forward tentatively with the score at 65. Marsh had dived low to his right to take the ball in front of first slip.

The ever-reliable Alan Knott, with a series of cover drives and nudges behind square, combined with Old to take the score to 78 before Lillee returned to bowl from the southern end. Old walked when he gloved a Lillee delivery to Marsh and at lunch England was 8–83. Knott's 60-minute spell at the crease ended three runs after the break when he was defeated by a faster ball and struck on the pads in front. Nine runs later, at 95, the innings ended as Lever chased a wide Lillee delivery and Marsh, running to his right, accepted the catch. Inexplicably, England was bowled out for 95.

Dennis Lillee had taken his best Test figures of 6–26 off 13.3 overs and Walker 4–54 off 15 overs. Lillee brought all his theatrics with him when he bowled. When he appealed he would stay down on his haunches for extended periods to emphasise his appeal. Umpire Max O'Connell has a take on the way that Lillee appealed. 'Dennis would pause for just a moment after the ball hit the batsman's pads and then dramatically swivel around and hold the appeal. It was all for the cameras.'

Gary Cosier thinks that the ways the Australians celebrated was nothing on what happens nowadays. 'Back then if you scored a ton you would raise your bat for a few seconds and then bring it down. There wasn't this sense of staging that there is now.'

Looking back at the footage, you can see the sense of celebration as more of a spill over of excitement than an act aimed at sending a message.

When the Australians left the field they ran to congratulate Rod Marsh, who, by catching Lever, his fourth catch of the innings, went to 188 Test victims, beating Wally Grout's record of 187. As he set the new world record, Marsh had a signed photograph of the keeper for the first Australian Test in 1877, Jack Blackham, in his pocket.

Amazingly, Australia led by 43 runs—a result that would have been considered unimaginable when the day began. Even when Thomson and Lillee had blitzed England two years before, their lowest score was 166 on a difficult Brisbane wicket. As Gary Cosier left the field he thought he would get the tap on the shoulder to open the batting. Although he was a middle-order batsman he had opened the innings at Shield level. That tap never came. Instead, Cosier would bat at number four.

As the Australians walked off the field, Greg Chappell walked past Kerry O'Keeffe and quietly had a word in his ear, 'Mate I want you to open. I want you to get your head down and play the best innings of your life. If you can get us through the new ball, we'll be okay.' Chappell reflected on the move in his book *Fierce Focus*:

> *I thought Kerry O'Keeffe competent enough to survive the new ball, then we'd have our normal batting intact. But I couldn't tell him yet. To say Kerry lacked self-confidence would be a generous view. I rarely saw another player who had so little self-confidence. With the ball he was the Anil Kumble of his day. He had a bounding stride and something that was a bit different, a lot of overspin and skid rather than side spin. With the bat he was known as Don Bradman...in the nets. He was technically solid, a good driver but outside the nets he seldom batted to his talent. Opening was a big job to ask of him, but the longer he had to think about it the worse it would be...To his credit he did play the innings of his life, surviving for nearly an hour.*

O'Keeffe felt a bit unnerved by the request but also inspired. Here he was thinking, 'I'm on a pair of ducks in the biggest match of all time and the skipper wants me to open.' O'Keeffe opened with Ian Davis and batted solidly, gliding the ball between the slips and gully to get off the mark. O'Keeffe, proved he had the straight-bat defence of an opener and made it to 14 before he leant forward to the second ball of Old's second over and the edge was taken by Willis at third slip.

Greg Chappell appeared at number three, probably due to Cosier's disappointing effort in the first innings. Stability was needed at the top of the order given the state of the match. Despite not making a mistake for 15 minutes, Chappell was bowled by Old for two, missing what appeared to be a straight delivery. Australia was again struggling at 2–40. Cosier arrived, unusually for him batting in an Australian cap, and this time determined not to repeat his mistake of the first innings. After twenty minutes of resisting and helping Davis to raise the score to 50, Lever pitched short and Cosier tried to hook from a standing position, the ball struck his glove and flew skywards for Alan Knott, running to take an easy chance.

After a shaky start where Walters was beaten outside off stump and repeatedly bounced, he responded with a cover drive for four. He and Davis stabilised the top order with the Australian opener looking very confident.

At tea the ACB chairman Bob Parish escorted Harold Larwood and Bill Voce to the centre. Voce took off his jacket and marked out his run and the crowd warmly applauded.

After tea one spectator decided he wanted to spend some time in the middle and ran a lap of the ground into the arms of a waiting policeman after being jeered and pelted with bottles and cans by the crowd.

In the final session Walters had a chance on 16 off Old. Willis in the gully dropped the straightforward chance. It was the first time that a chance had gone down. Walters responded by clipping Underwood past point for two. Davis and Walters started playing assuredly with a series of back-foot drives that indicated the wicket was evening out.

Australia 138 and 3–104 (Davis 45, Walters 32) England 95 Attendance 62,505

DAY TWO REFLECTIONS

Marsh recalled of the first two days: 'The drama was unbelievable and it was an amazing game there were so many twists and turns and the catching on both sides was really memorable.'

The pundits were wondering why it was that both teams had collapsed on the first two days? Was it the pressure of the occasion?

Greg Chappell certainly thought so. 'The real destroyer has been the rare pressure...I don't think Tony Greig or myself really thought that the festivities and atmosphere of this celebration would affect our players to this degree.'

Yet, it could be argued that the bowling line-ups and fielders had performed incredibly well under pressure. Barely a chance went down in two days and the ability of the bowlers to make the most out of a first-day wicket was exceptional.

Max Walker drew inspiration from being the only Melbourne Cricket Club player in the match while English writer Crawford White described the batting by both sides in the first innings as 'appalling by any Test standards'.

In his brief first innings of just four runs Derek Randall had felt the tension at the ground. He may have doffed his cap to Dennis Lillee but he felt ill at ease. 'I think my doffing of my cap upset him a bit that particular day. I didn't have to say much he finished up within two feet of me and he was lost for words.' Lillee was becoming frustrated bowling at Randall, as he later wrote in *Lillee: An Autobiography*:

> *Randall, doffing his cap and smiling at us and making remarks such as, 'That was a good one Mr Lillee.' When I knocked him over he would just pick himself up, dust himself down and then grin down the wicket at me. He also moved around the crease just before actually playing the ball. It got so much that in the end I snarled at him. 'Stand still! It's so much harder to hit a moving target.' It was true and he never kept still. But I did hit him once, a sickening blow on the head, but again he just grinned and said later 'I was lucky. If it had hit me anywhere else it would have probably killed me but as it hit me on the side of the head it wasn't too bad.' I laughed out loud at that comment.*

Hundreds of thousands of English Sunday papers had to be pulped because the late news of England's collapse wiped out earlier stories of how Australia had all but lost the match. It was a strange start to the match.

Victoria's captain, Richie Robinson, had been called in to act as thirteenth man, given Ray Bright now had to field for the injured Rick McCosker. Bright, who had occasionally experienced crowds of several thousand during Sheffield Shield matches, remembers the wall of sound he experienced as he walked on to the MCG that first day. 'I felt a bit overawed initially and then settled down. I didn't have a lot to do mainly fielding in the gully and mid-on and mid-off.'

As the Test wore on it was obvious that Gary Gilmour's gout, that had caused problems throughout the season, had again flared up.

Greg Chappell recalled that the conditions at the start of the second day were tougher than the first:

> The pitch had started to harden up and while it was a slow seamer on the first day, on the second day...while the pitch was not doing as much what it did do was quicker. We bowled a good length which challenged England. In some ways it was probably better that we didn't get too many more runs than we did as we may have lost the chance to bowl at them in the friendly conditions. Had we battled through to lunch on the second day we might have been in a bit more trouble.

If Australia had managed to battle it out through to lunch on the second day, by the second session the pitch would have flattened out sufficiently for England to set a very large total.

As Gary Cosier sat in the Australian dressing room he wondered how he had managed to be dismissed twice by Lever in the same manner:

> I'd played against Willis before for South Australia and scored a hundred when I did but I hadn't faced John Lever. It was unbelievable that just 24 hours after what happened in the first innings I did it again. I batted 34 minutes for four runs and didn't play a false shot and thought I was

through the worst of it and then all of a sudden Lever bowls
a bouncer and I hit it and the ball hits my gloves again it
was the worst feeling and still is now.

For Cosier the choice of stroke was 'just a reaction'. In his mind he'd put the shot away after falling victim to Imran's bouncer the season before. It sounds as if it was something that he had tried to avoid so much he ended up doing it. 'I have no answer for why I did it.' In Cosier's defence, out of the 13 leading Australian bowlers of the 1976–77 summer, only three were left-handers (Dymock, Gilmour and Attenborough) and none of these had the pace of Lever.

One aspect of the day that stuck in Cosier's mind was the presence of promotional girls in the dressing room during the day's play. When he was dismissed in the second innings and went downstairs to get changed there were girls dressed as Little Bo Peep sitting with the players in the viewing room and Cosier didn't know why they were there. 'They weren't in the room when I went out to bat. There had never ever been women in the dressing room sitting with the players.' Cosier later thought that, as times were changing (he was unaware of the Packer signings at the time), perhaps there had been a relaxing of the usual dressing room rules. 'Can you imagine Ian Chappell allowing three girls dressed as Miss Bo Peep in the Australian dressing room?' It was a hint of what was to come. When Wayne Daniel hit Mick Malone for a six at VFL Park to win the match during World Series Cricket in 1978 the television cameras panned to the celebrations in the West Indies dressing room where women in red and white uniforms scampered for the door.

The crowd for the second day's play was listed as 62,505. Some Australian players thought that the crowd was much bigger. Max Walker who had played in front of a crowd of 90,000 at the MCG thought the crowd was closer to 85,000.

CHAPTER

DAY THREE

Monday 14 March, the Labour Day holiday. Again blue skies as Australia resumed at 3–104 with Davis and Walters wanting to continue to make amends for their first innings failures.

They did, with Davis excelling with well timed back-foot drives, while Walters drove and pulled the ball with distinction. When Davis brought up his 50 with an exquisitely timed back-foot stroke he was the first batsman of the match to reach the milestone.

Davis was the first to go, caught behind off Greig to Knott. For the first time in his innings of 68 he showed uncertainty as he hung his bat out to catch the edge. Greig, wearing a neck tie, celebrated the breakthrough by punching the air.

Enter David Hookes with the score at 4–132. Greig could sense a vulnerability in the Australian batting line up that had looked so much more assured in the second innings.

Hookes struggled initially with Greig's medium pacers that had the left-hander beaten outside off stump, sparring at deliveries he should have left alone.

Despite the difficulties, Hookes and Walters added 50 in a little over an hour with Hookes scoring 36. Walters displayed his class with some strong drives off the back foot.

At lunch Australia had made it to 4–186.

At the time, New Zealand cricket was only just starting to edge its way into the Australian cricket fans' consciousness but at least there was a lunch-time, Wrigley's sponsored exhibition mile race featuring 1976 New Zealand Olympic champion John Walker, which he won in 4 minutes 5.4 seconds. He sped by his opponents with his black singlet adorned with the silver fern.

In the first over after the break Walters fell to Greig for 66, to a diving one-handed catch from Alan Knott, and the chance to bowl Australia out for an attainable target presented. Marsh swiped tentatively, initially, before steadying. He was millimetres away from being bowled off Underwood, attempting a crude sweep.

Greig had positioned himself at silly point off Underwood's bowling to get into Hookes ear, which he did each delivery. 'When are your balls going to drop sonny?

Greig later admitted he was rebuked by umpire Tom Brooks, 'Cool it, he's just a youngster.'

The England captain continued haranguing Hookes, regardless.

The next over, when Greig decided to bowl off spin, Hookes decided to take revenge for the verbal lashing he had been receiving. Batting at the southern end, he was content to defend the first two balls from Greig's over. With the game so evenly poised the public holiday crowd of more than 55,000 had quietened. That was soon to change. Greig's third ball was a well flighted off break that Hookes belted over the bowler's head to the extra cover boundary, one bounce into the picket fence.

Frank Tyson, commentating, said: 'Hookes is certainly not frightened to hit the ball.'

The next ball as a quicker one down the leg side. Hookes pirouetted like a ballerina and gracefully sent the ball down to the deep fine leg fence. The previously quiet crowd started shrieking like a grand final audience.

In the Australian dressing room there were some concerns that Hookes might lose his head. Gary Gilmour, as next man in, kept saying to himself, 'settle down, settle down.' Cosier responded, 'You've got no chance of him settling down once he starts he's off.'

The mood in the Australian dressing room became more buoyant with each boundary that Hookes struck. There was a certain glee at the fact that it was the England captain Tony Greig on the receiving end of the mauling.

The next shot was a picture perfect cover drive sent shooting to the extra cover boundary. It was a controlled shot of complete authority. Hookes wandered out to pat down the pitch as if to inform Greig where he would like the next ball delivered.

The fourth ball, and the stroke to bring up his 50, was an elegant push in front of square. For what barely looked a deflection from Hookes' bat the ball sped to the boundary. Hookes briefly took off his cap and raised his bandaged bat to the crowd's standing ovation .and then, put his cap back on and brought his bat down as if he meant to say that this was only the beginning.

The fifth ball, courtesy of a poised and graceful cover drive that carried 90 metres before dropping into the gutter ahead of a pursuing fieldsman, carried Hookes from 36 to 56 in five balls. The crowd, by then, was in a state of pandemonium.

Hookes looked as if he might make it six fours in one over, driving Greig's final ball powerfully into the covers but, Randall was there to field it.

As much as Rick McCosker's Test match was about bravery and sacrifice for the team, David Hookes' five fours in a row off Tony Greig were a statement of the audacity of youth.

Greg Chappell: 'That was the turning point of the Test match as far as I was concerned…we knew then that any gremlins in the wicket had gone and from here on it was going to be a good wicket to bat on.'

For Sir Donald Bradman it was as if Frank Woolley had been reborn for five balls.

Then just as suddenly as this amazing display of stroke play arrived, it ended.

With great anticlimax and with no addition to his score Hookes was caught at short leg, off Underwood. Greig couldn't help himself, giving Hookes a send-off. 'Piss off', said Greig.

Hookes responded in an equally aggressive manner: 'At least I'm an

Australian playing for Australia and not a…South African playing for England.'

(After play, Tony Greig carried a long neck bottle of beer into the Australian dressing room to share with Hookes, with his first comments being, 'well played'.)

A standing ovation followed for Hookes as the crowd appreciated seeing the first time in the match when the bat had gained mastery of the ball.

'What a superb innings. I'm sure we have seen a champion of the future', exclaimed ABC special comments man, Paul Sheahan.

With the score at 6–244, Gilmour joined Marsh. Marsh made the most of the momentum gained by Hookes when he square cut Underwood past point for four to bring up the 250. After hooking a boundary, Gilmour was yorked by Lever and was out for 16. Marsh and Lillee now faced the prospect of the batting through the second new ball. Lillee appeared to relish the role, lofting Old for successive deliveries over backward square leg. Marsh's straight drive off Old for four had the look of a batsman determined to take control of the situation. He reached 50 in just 77 balls.

When Lillee was caught by Amiss in the covers off Old, Australia's eighth-wicket stand of 76 in 87 minutes had ended. Lillee was out for 25 and Australia was 8–353. The stand must have just about broken England's will as the match appeared to be sailing out of their control with the lead at 396.

One of the most extraordinary events on the cricket field was the appearance of a bandaged faced Rick McCosker, who came out to bat with Kerry O'Keeffe as his runner. Bandages encircled him from throat to scalp, with the cap sitting almost as an add-on on top of his head.

Hardly believing his eyes commentator Norman May had surprise in his voice, 'Here's McCosker swathed in bandages with Marsh approaching his century.

McCosker described the moment as 'a spine tingling magic moment that helped me and gave me the inspiration…I could tell that these guys understood what I was trying to do.'

Max Walker in the Australian dressing room slid the glass windows back so that the Australians could hear the crowd, 'Listen to this.' 'He knew full well that he would be bowled a bouncer first up. It takes a different sort of courage…to do that.'

'Waltzing McCosker, Waltzing McCosker, you'll come a Waltzing McCosker with me.' The sound of the crowd cheering Australia's injured opening batsman sent a shiver up the spine of the Australian team members, who clearly remember the incident today.

As soon as Tony Greig saw McCosker walking out to bat he went over to speak with Willis, 'Let him have it. If he wants to come out here then that's the way it is', was Greig's directive. In other words, bowl short and quick at him.

Max O'Connell standing at the bowler's end remembers Bob Willis saying to McCosker as he walked in to bat, 'Short one, slow down the leg side.'

Marsh told McCosker he didn't have to stay out there; he could go off at any moment. McCosker simply told him to bugger off and that he was there to see Marsh get his hundred. The fact that Marsh on 82 and looked set to score a century no doubt inspired McCosker to bat on.

Twice McCosker hooked Lever to the fence. For almost an hour McCosker batted for 17 runs. At Stumps with Marsh on 95, Australia led by 430. Despite ordering his bowlers to bounce McCosker Greig said he 'would have hated Rick to be hit. It would have caused a riot had he been struck on the face again.'

McCosker later admitted. 'It made me realise what Test cricket is all about.'

Greg Chappell remembers:

> There wasn't a lot of discussion around it (the idea of McCosker batting again). We didn't expect him to bat again and I didn't talk to him about the idea. He was the one who came up and offered to bat. I don't think I would have contemplated raising the subject with him, but he was the one who said he wanted to bat which says a

lot about him as an individual and the feeling about the Test match. It was an important occasion and we wanted to give ourselves a chance of winning the Test match and Rick being the quintessential team man insisted he bat. It required the doctors cut the wiring to his jaw so that if anything happened and he vomited he could open his mouth so he wouldn't choke.

While there was great bravery on the field some unruly behaviour in the crowd spoiled the day for some fans. Twenty-one people were charged by police with offences including assault, drunk and disorderly behaviour, resisting arrest and assaulting police.

Australia 138 and 8–387 (Marsh 95, McCosker 17) England 95 Attendance 55,399

DAY THREE REFLECTIONS

Australian captain Greg Chappell watched the gushing sentiment associated with the match with a growing apprehension that turned into anger. He was moved to declare:

The constant criticism in the press on radio and television and among the large group of former players that has been directed at both teams over the past few days. I am sick to the back teeth of hearing these so called experts declaring both the English and Australian Test sides as sub-standard. The comparison with teams of the past of is both misleading and grossly unfair.

Chappell pointed out the Australian batsmen of the 1930s were humbled in the second Test in Sydney in 1936–37 for 80 and that Hutton, Compton and Yardley were bowled out for 51 at the Oval in 1948. 'This Centenary Test is one of the hardest matches I have played in with unbelievable pressure applied from both sides from the start.'

There are few moments in a Test match that so captivate the audience that they feel they are being drawn to it like some giant magnet drawing in iron filings. That though was the case when David Hookes faced up to Tony Greig on day three of the Centenary Test.

Greg Chappell saw Hookes' five fours in a row as crucial to Australia's morale. 'It made us realise that it was now a pretty good wicket and that we really needed to make some runs to win the match.'

The Centenary Test means different things to different people. Barry Gibbs a former South Australian cricket association CEO and a Victorian who was living in Melbourne in 1977 had a delightful story to share of he and his wife Peg rushing to get to the MCG to see the new SA-batting sensation on day three of the match. They were delayed in leaving because Peg took some time to get ready and they then struck every red traffic light on the way to the ground. After finally arriving they were redirected to the furthest point of the Jolimont car park, about a kilometre from the entrance gate. Gibbs feverishly made his way to the gate with his wife trailing behind.

The roars of the crowd became louder and louder. Gibbs wrote in *My Cricket Journey* about what happened next:

> *Then came an eruption which I can only compare with the fantastic sound which echoes around the MCG when the mighty blues burst onto the arena.*
>
> *I was just about to enter the ground...No problems I thought no 'out' noise, so Hookesy must still be at the crease. As we made our way to our seats through the maze of stairs, there was a groan—now that was the reaction of the Aussie batsman getting out. Sure enough we reached our seats just in time to see Hookes trudging off to a standing ovation.*

Ian Davis reflected on his day at the crease and thought he had rarely played better:

The second innings of the Centenary Test was the best innings in my career. It was an important innings, I was proud of that innings. I had been shocked at the pace of Willis...it was the toughest Test I played in. I felt like I'd been in a war there was that much sledging.

McCosker having spent the last two days listening to the match unfold from his hospital bed was back sitting in the Australian change room as the third afternoon wore on:

Greg Chappell came up to me and asked if I wanted to bat again and I said yes that I did...it was just a matter of when was an opportune time to go in. As far as I was concerned it was always going to happen...I felt okay... bravery didn't really come into it. There were a couple of very good reasons for me to want to bat again. One was that this was the most significant game of cricket ever in cricket history apart from the 1877 Test and I wanted to be a part of it and do whatever I could. The second was that the wicket had become very flat and England had a very good batting side and we needed more runs to build up a very big second innings. Rod Marsh was also getting close to his maiden Test century and we wanted to do all we could to help him get there.

Any criticism of Greg Chappell allowing McCosker to bat again was dismissed by Chappell on ABC radio on the rest day. 'Rick was passed by the doctors as being fit to bat and it was good for him to go out and bat... Rick said he was well aware of the dangers.'

SOME PLAYERS DECIDE

After stumps the day before the rest day, umpires Brooks and O'Connell sensed some unease in the silence that they experienced when they walked into the dressing rooms. They concluded that the players must have been criticising their umpiring. 'We had no idea what was going on. If there were any whispers about Packer we hadn't heard them.' O'Connell later admitted.

Austin Robertson's presence had been frequent in the Australian dressing room and there he was again. This time he was informing Max Walker that a number of other members of the team had signed up to World Series Cricket and invited him to join the group. Walker wouldn't decide on it until he had spoken to Lillee, which he did when they walked back to the Hilton hotel together that night, where another long discussion followed.

The next morning, on the rest day, as he played with his eighteen-month old son Tristan, Walker happily signed both copies of the contract. Max Walker recalled the contract presented to the players: 'In effect it said 55 days of your life play World Series Cricket. The very best players in the world. You are able to earn some money.'

The rest day of the Centenary Test was anything but for some Australian players who were making up their minds as to whether to sign up with Kerry Packer's cricket venture.

For some the decision would be delayed. Greg Chappell, who had already decided, chose to delay signing with Kerry Packer until weeks after the Centenary Test. The fact that players were being approached during the match, according to Chappell, was no great distraction:

> *You have to understand that this had been going on for quite some time. We had been having discussions with the Board for most of my Test career about improving relationships, improving the situation for players which was not just around money, it was around respect and treating us like first-class citizens, taking our opinion on tours and tour conditions.*

Chappell had experienced the hectic nature of two England tours (In 1972 they played five Tests, three one-day internationals and 23 other first-class games) where they had to zigzag across the country. Chappell thought that taking in some feedback from players would have made for less rushed and better organised tours. He knew full well the ACB would pass the responsibility off onto the MCC for organising the tour, but the lack of thought revealed much about how much cricket administrators cared for their charges.

The decision was made easier for Greg Chappell who had a young family, a business and, as one of Australia's top Test cricketer, wasn't being paid much. He could no longer afford to be away for six months of the year on overseas cricket tours. Most Test cricketers long for one tour of England but, by 1977, Chappell was about to embark on his third and last:

> I was already thinking about scaling back my cricket touring. The Packer business wasn't a big deal from my point of view. I was focused on the Centenary Test and looking forward to the tour of England.

Chappell was of the understanding that once Austin Robertson and John Cornell had signed the players they wanted, Kerry Packer was going to go to the Board and negotiate a broadcasting rights deal. 'There was still a lot to be decided and the expectation wasn't that there was to be any great schism.'

Rick McCosker, broken jaw and all, was invited to join but paused to decide after talking with his wife. There were other matters to attend to, namely his injury and also the end of this historic match. He knew there would be plenty of time to sign and that if they had asked him most of the side would have been asked.

It was amazing that news of the Packer signings didn't leak given the number of receptions where so many players were present at once.

CHAPTER XVII

A DINNER AND A REST DAY

The Australian Cricket Board dinner was held on the Monday evening before the rest day. As Frank Tyson noted in his book, *The Centenary Test*:

> *The Monday evening was devoted to the highlight of the Centenary Test's social calendar, the Australian Cricket Board dinner held in honour of both a hundred years of Test cricket and the surviving participants of previous England–Australia games...when the guests passed into the dining room to take their seats, they created cricket history, there has never been and probably will never be again, such a galaxy of sporting talents sitting down to a meal together.*

The dinner was described as a dignified yet glamorous occasion. The players and administrators passed an ice sculpture of an Ashes urn as they gathered before the dinner in the foyer of the Hilton hotel's banquet room.

I wonder how some of the Australian players who had signed with Packer, or were about to, felt being part of this great celebration. What they were about to do was to fly in the face of all the history that was being presented that night and join a privately sponsored competition directly at odds with the wishes of the Australian Cricket Board. If there was any guilt it would have been quickly appeased as they looked around the vast Hilton ball room, where the function was held, and noted that the ACB had spared no expense when it came to providing such a lavish meal in such refined surrounds. Ian and Greg Chappell had both asked for a modest pay rise for their players, just so they could earn enough to keep playing the game, and had been rebuffed, mainly by Sir Donald Bradman, the man at the centre of the ACB dinner and who was giving the key note speech.

The Chairman of the Australian Cricket Board Bob Parish welcomed the guests while Freddie Brown the Chairman of the UK Cricket Council provided a response and a gift of a silver salver inscribed with the names of every living England player who had been invited to attend the Centenary Test.

Sir Donald Bradman gave a witty and intelligent speech concentrating on Test cricket up until the Second World War while carefully passing over the details of the 1932–33 Bodyline Series. An example of the humour and detail spread throughout the talk was Bradman's observation:

> In 1873, the famous Dr WG Grace was persuaded to bring a team to Australia. They had to change ships at Colombo and took 50 times as long to get there as the Concorde now does. I don't think WG minded very much as he was on his honeymoon. In addition, as an amateur he also had the attraction that not only his expenses but also those of his wife were paid and he himself received the equivalent of $30,000 in today's currency.

He also went on to remind the audience of Australia's finest statistician Roy Webber's claim that the 1877 Test should not have been called a Test match contending that it was not England's best side but as Bradman went on:

> If this was the only the only criterion, many subsequent matches could be challenged in similar grounds—the most publicised instance being when six of Australia's leading players refused to go to England in 1912 because they

couldn't have the manager of their choice. But perhaps the greatest significance is that in the 1885 Murdoch captained Australia in the First Test but following a dispute between the administrators and players about remuneration, the whole team was dropped and a new 11 picked for the second test.

While Bradman was unaware of it many of Australia's players were busy defecting to Kerry Packer's World's Series Cricket. His theory that you don't necessarily need the best teams to play for a match to be considered a test match would soon be well and truly tested.

With the advent of World Series Cricket where the best of the Australia side were unavailable, Bradman would now witness Australia second and at times third elevens playing of for prestigious trophies such as Ashes and the Sir Frank Worrell trophy.

Bradman made references to the one-day knock out games—or limited overs cricket, saying that they:

...have added new dimensions bring good and bad features... undoubtedly they must take some responsibility for the decline in the use of slow leg spinners, a development which worries me greatly.

The potential of its ability to draw in massive crowds would be exploited by Kerry Packer and his day–night cricket during World Series Cricket but would not be acknowledged by the Australian Cricket Board.

What stands out in Bradman's speech is his eye for historical detail. The fact that:

Greg Chappell throughout his career had to defend a set of stumps one inch higher and 12 per cent wider, than the stumps Trumper had to guard. He had to bat against a smaller ball and cope with a more difficult lbw rule. On the

other hand, Trumper had to bat on uncovered wickets. How
can anyone possibly equate those differences?

This was a match that had the eyes of the nation on it. The rest day provided a chance for everyone to take in what had already happened. A frenetic first innings for both teams, the batting sides falling apart in challenging conditions. Then the drying of the wicket and an Australia fightback with the bat. It was like witnessing two games in one. This was a match that for many had a water cooler effect, where people gathered in groups chatting around the water cooler at work. Such was its hold on the nation. This was a different time. There was no social media and most people got their news from either newspapers or radio and television. We also hadn't seen the break out of other less mainstream sports such as soccer or basketball. Cricket was the national sport of the country in 1977. Its characters loomed large across all media to the point where it almost felt as if you knew the players.

In this day and age of the instant gratification of Twenty20 cricket it is easy to forget just how one single Test match, seen by many as a mere exhibition match, could have gained the attention across the country that it did. The Australian cricket public had been mesmerised by the events shown live across the country on two different television networks (Channels Two and Ten as well as radio coverage on the ABC and other commercial broadcasters). State broadsheet and tabloids and the national paper, *The Australian,* covered the match in detail, it was as if for a while that the country had little else to talk about or do than consider how the match might turn out.

The Rest day was held on Tuesday 15 March, the exact anniversary of the first Test between Australia and England.

Despite the rain, a number of the Centenary Test guests relaxed around the Hilton hotel's swimming pool. At lunch time in the Lounge Bar former England fast bowler Frank Tyson heard Eddie Paynter bemoaning the fact that Australians froze their beer until it was almost solid. A waiter placed a bottle under the running water of a hot tap and opened it, pouring a foaming glass for Paynter. 'Eeh that's lovely,' replied the Lancastrian with a broad smile.

There was little that couldn't be done to make the guests feel at home.

England batsman Derek Randall was so consumed by the occasion he spent much of the rest day hanging around the Hilton hotel while others relaxed in various pubs across the city or chose the more active practice of a game of golf. Godfrey Evans and Denis Compton spent a day at the Kilmore Trotting meeting Test cricketers young and old spread themselves around many beautiful and wooded golf courses of Melbourne's sand belt, their ages varying as widely as their handicaps.

Dennis Lillee and Rod Marsh went over to the Punt Road oval where they wore the Richmond footy club jumpers and trained with some of the Tiger stars including Kevin Sheedy and Barry Richardson, at times out bumping and out marking them. It's worth comparing what the response might be in the modern game if the star opening bowler and wicketkeeper were involved in training that involved physical contact with elite level Australian Rules footballers.

The move by Lillee seemed to dispel rumours that he had visited a specialist for his back during the Test and that he wouldn't be touring England. John Arlott noted that several times in this match he was plainly labouring as he came up to his delivery stride.

A somewhat relieved David Hookes, who had stepped up in one of the most high pressure matches of all time, enjoyed a peaceful rest day on the golf course. He was yet to be approached by Packer's acolytes but those approaches would come soon enough. Hookes was to become of the poster boys for World Series Cricket and an integral part of Packer's cricketing revolution.

Greg Chappell and Gary Cosier slipped into an out-of-the way pub in town to have some peace and quiet. But even there everyone was talking cricket and soon they were recognised and signing autographs.

Ian Davis found he was in demand from Packer's acolytes. On the rest day, sleeping in his hotel room, Davis fielded a phone call from Austin Robertson, who he'd met in New Zealand: 'I need to see you. I will pick you up in a limo in one hour and take you to the Old Windsor Hotel.'

A bemused Davis enquired as to what it was all about. Robertson replied, 'No this is really important, you have no idea how important this is, I really need to see you.'

Robertson raced Davis down to the Windsor and they took the back lift and walked straight into a room where John Cornell was waiting:

> They said they were forming World Series Cricket with Kerry Packer and Ian Chappell wanted me to be part of the Australian side. I was told it was a chance to make a bit of money and that I would be paid more than I was now. They said I'd still be able to play Test cricket. It would only be a two- or three-month thing…they said I had to swear to secrecy and that I had to let them know in a week what I was going to do.

A slightly stunned Ian Davis left the room stunned by what he had heard but convinced he would sign.

As Frank Tyson put it, 'the rest day was defused of repose at 5.30 pm when the social round began in the form of a cocktail party given by Sir Lenox Hewitt, chairman of Qantas airlines.'

For Greg Chappell, who attended every function throughout the Test, it was a once in a lifetime chance to catch up and meet some of the great Australian and England players of the past:

> My first Test matches were representing England playing in the backyard against my older brother (Ian) who was Australia, which meant I was England. I had been batting for some of these fellows such as Colin Cowdrey, Tom Graveney and Peter May and was keen to meet them. Also meeting Harold Larwood who had played against my grandfather was fascinating.

CHAPTER

XVIII

Day Four

Day four loomed as critical for Australia to set a total for England to chase. Greg Chappell was interviewed that morning on ABC radio before play, 'We'll attempt to bat on until Rod Marsh gets his century, for about an hour or so.'

Australia began the day leading by 430 and batted on for one hour before Greg Chappell declared. Marsh took 15 minutes to reach his ton. McCosker's effort had given Marsh the chance to score a century, the first by an Australian wicketkeeper against England in a Test match. Marsh reached the milestone with a leg-glanced single from Willis who shook Marsh by the hand as the Australian wicket keeper ran to his end to complete the single.

'A wicket keeping record for Australia and now a batting record for Australia, the first man in history as an Australian keeper to get a century in a test (against England) and he's done it in the Centenary.' The ABC's Norman May told us.

As Marsh celebrated his hundred he appeared to wave away Keith Fletcher, who was clapping the Australian keeper. It gave some indication as to how Marsh and his team-mates viewed Fletcher—as someone who struggled in Australian conditions.

Marsh had approached the milestone against England on two previous occasions. In Melbourne in 1971 he scored a 92 not out against Illingworth's tourists and was only kept away from his century by his captain, Lawry's, declaration. The next year he hit a rapid fire 91 in the first Test at Old Trafford before succumbing caught behind.

McCosker made 25 before he struck out at Old and Greig took the catch at midwicket. Lillee described McCosker's efforts as:

> ...one of the greatest things I've seen in a Test match... we really needed a few more runs to make it very hard for England and for us to set them a reasonable total. The bowler who was charging in at the other end was none other than the bloke who had decked him in the first innings, Bob Willis. And it was two or three bouncers in the first dozen deliveries which the MCG crowd gave the raspberry to.

For 42 minutes his partnership with Marsh had added 57, taking Australia 287 runs ahead of England. At noon Greg Chappell closed the innings at 9–419, giving England five-and-a-half sessions to chase 462. Marsh was undefeated on 110 in 297 minutes off 175 deliveries and with ten fours. Max Walker remained eight not out

Woolmer and Brearley opened the England innings, with both batsmen determined to make up for first innings failures. For Woolmer this meant taking anything dangerous from Lillee on the body while Brearley played and missed, sparring outside off stump. Woolmer was the first to go, lbw to Walker playing back to a ball that kept low. At lunch England was 1–28. Randall and Brearley then added 85 runs between lunch and tea without being separated. Brearley later said on Lillee:

> He bowled straighter as the match went on and the bounce was getting lower then bowling more for bowled and lbw. He could bowl to a 7–2 off side field and give you nothing to play to leg and very few balls to leave safely. He was fast and swung the ball.

Gilmour replaced Lillee after the break but with little effect. His first three deliveries were no balls and his four overs cost 29 runs. Randall was the most punishing on Gilmour, stroking him to the off-side fence off both the back and front foot.

Gilmour was suffering an injury to his left toe and Australia was left with only three front-line bowlers, Lillee, Walker and O'Keeffe. For Gilmour it was the last time he would bowl in a test match.

Tony Greig, fearing that Randall would fade from Test cricket, gave him a pep talk before his innings. Greig had noticed that Randall had made a number of starts but not gone on with it:

> *I told him that if he kept making starts and that was all that the critics would say that he wasn't cut out for Test cricket and this might be the last time he played for England. He really had to convert starts into a big score.*

Lillee was testing Randall's fortitude. In one over he bowled six bouncers. The crowd loved it and Randall stood and delivered, pulling Lillee through midwicket for four. Randall was combining the orthodox with the unconventional when he thrashed at one ball outside off stump and was then dropped in the gully by O'Keeffe the next ball. Leaving a delivery over middle stump he then hit another bouncer past point for four.

Randall, despite being a flurry of movement in between deliveries—repeatedly touching his pads, cap and gloves—showed that he was not afraid of Lillee by hitting him in front of square leg for four. He also simply glared back when Lillee thundered down the pitch on full follow through, giving Randall one of his heated glares. Randall at times provoked Lillee, pointing mockingly at the wicket as if to suggest the great fast bowler should improve his direction. Brearley lasted until the first over after tea when he pushed forward to a Lillee delivery that came back and was out lbw for 43. England was 2–113.

The idea of another encounter between Amiss and Lillee had the outer roaring; this was a contest the wicket-hungry Australian crowds loved. Amiss who had been pushed down to bat at number four did not relish the prospect:

It hadn't been an easy time for me in Australia in 1974–75 when I struggled to get any runs at all against Lillee. Randall took a fair bit of the strike against him early on and I ended up facing more of Max Walker and Kerry O'Keeffe which suited me.

O'Keeffe, who was finding the wicket unsympathetic to spin, relied on dip in the flight of his deliveries to twice have chances from Amiss go to ground. (One to Hookes at third slip, the other short leg, where Cosier fumbled.) The misses were a significant let off; by stumps Randall was 87 and Amiss was on 34. England was placed at 2–191.

With Randall on the verge of a century in his first Test match in Australia, people began asking about him. Bill O'Reilly, writing in *The Sydney Morning Herald,* revealed that England's new hero didn't play cricket as a schoolboy. 'Randall was destined to take up the usual coalmining job that falls so easily to the lot of the Midland boys who live in the Nottinghamshire area.'

That night the Melbourne Cricket Club held its special commemoration, celebrating past players and celebrating its link with the Marylebone Cricket Club. Gifts were exchanged between the two presidents Sir Albert Chadwick and Mr WH Webster while Judy Boyd had the task of collecting the autographs of every person in the room on the three menus, one for Lord's, one for the Club and a spare. Despite it taking her all night the finished the task just as the guests were starting to leave—only a frantic dash secured signatures from the departing Bradman.

Australia 138 and 9–419, England 95 and 2–191 Attendance 37,648

DAY FOUR REFLECTIONS
Tony Greig later said:

We always thought Marsh was a bit of a slogger but on that day he really did turn it on...I remember Knotty coming to me and saying do you realise how significant this is? Marsh's innings and the partnerships he had with other players really swung the match.

Rod Marsh who had just struck his third hundred yet first against England recalled the tension on the players throughout the match but dismissed his achievement of scoring a century; 'with five down and the wicket playing easier and McCosker's jaw wired up it was vital that I made a few.'

Colin Cowdrey thought that with eight wickets in hand the batsmen only needed 90 per session, a task he thought they could achieve on a slow, easy-paced pitch.

Even Lillee was pessimistic in his newspaper column, 'I'm beginning to worry whether we can get out of it.'

Dennis Amiss was relieved that he had made a start despite his early sense of unease:

I enjoyed batting in Melbourne and had made runs there in the last series (90). The wicket was slower and lower, more like an English wicket I was feeling that if Arkle and I could stay around with the wicket getting easier and easier to bat on we might make a fist of it.

There was also a connection between Randall and Amiss, who had been roommates on the tour to India. Randall remembered how Amiss had helped him settle before his first Test in India. 'Familiar with virtually every cricketing country in the world…'Sacker' was a sensible and uncomplicated man to be with and did his best to take my mind off the following day.'

Amiss thought that if they could get through the first session unscathed they were a real chance to win the match.

With Randall undefeated on 87 it gave *The Daily Mail's* Alex Bannister pause for thought, 'I have never seen Derek bat better…he has laid bare the Australian secret that they are virtually a two man bowling side.'

Words that would later come back to haunt the English press man.

CHAPTER

DAY FIVE

Tony Greig was interviewed by ABC radio on the final day of the match with England chasing down a world record to win:

> *We know it's a huge task ahead of us today but cricket is a funny game and this game has gone in so many directions… history is there to be changed and there is always a first time. The first two hours of the game are the most crucial. There is always a first time.*

Greig rebuffed suggestions that Australia was allowing England to keep batting to ensure the Queen's visit

The final day of the Centenary Test began with a question mark over the head of Dennis Lillee. It had been noted that he had struggled on the fourth afternoon and also with the forthcoming side to England to be announced after the match *The Age* reported that Lillee had yet to inform the selectors of his availability.

Even with the new ball not due for 13 overs, it was Lillee who opened the bowling with O'Keeffe. Randall and Amiss looked assured picking up singles and the odd boundary, keeping the Australian fielders alert. After almost four hours at the crease Randall cut Lillee to the fence for four to bring up his century. It had taken him 233 minutes and 173 balls including ten fours.

Randall's use of unorthodox strokes—at one stage almost tennis swiping a Lillee short ball to mid-off—frustrated Lillee who responded with a bouncer that Randall tried to duck away from but he was struck on the back of his head. The ball rebounded to Lillee who caught it, while Randall, having fallen over simply hoisted himself up again. (Lillee had been promising to knock Randall's cap off for the entire innings.)

Chappell and Lillee bowled to contain but still Randall and Amiss put on 46 in the first hour. Amiss at this stage looked more comfortable than his partner who, on 103, edged O'Keeffe into his pads to Gilmour, who failed to take the chance. Then Lillee thought he had Randall caught behind but Max O'Connell ruled not out, while the English batsman rubbed his shoulder to indicate that was where the ball struck.

Australia took the new ball and Walker was hit for 15 off two overs. Lillee by now was bowling from ten paces.

At lunch England's deficit was 196.

At the break it was announced that Lillee was not available for the tour of England after X-rays had indicated that old stress fractures had reopened and that he would be taking a break from the rigours of Test cricket.

Randall opened aggressively after lunch; in three balls he took ten runs off Lillee. Chappell, bowling from the other end, managed to sneak a ball through Amiss' defences with one that kept low.

Amiss who had felt as good as he ever had in Australia was shattered to have been dismissed. He had just played and missed, and then missed an opportunity to get off strike after squeezing a ball into the covers:

> *I could just feel my concentration going and should have pulled myself up. We were travelling well and on track to chase the total. If Randall and I had been able to bat for a bit longer it would have made the run chase much more achievable.*

Amiss was gone for 64 and his partnership with Randall was 166. Amiss had played a crucial sheet anchor role for Randall to go about scoring freely.

As soon as Amiss was out Randall gave a head-high chance to Cosier at mid wicket, who missed the chance.

Keith Fletcher's wretched match continued when he was caught behind off Lillee. England had lost 2–11 chasing another 173 with six wickets in hand. Tony Greig made his intentions clear hitting Lillee for two fours through the covers. In four overs England had hit Lillee for 41 runs.

Greg Chappell's niggling medium pacers were proving more economical conceding just seven runs in five overs. When Randall edged and Marsh took the chance the Australians were jubilant as this was the breakthrough they had been seeking. As Greg Chappell ran to Marsh he could see his keeper shaking his head and crossing his arms as if to indicate Randall wasn't out.

'What do you mean he's not out asked Chappell? 'He didn't hit it', Marsh replied. 'Well Tom Brooks gave it out that's enough for me.' 'No, it didn't carry'. 'Well that's a bit different', replied Chappell.

All around the MCG spectators applauded the Australian wicketkeeper for his action.

The exchange reflects an interesting ethical debate in cricketing circles. That is, that it is okay to successfully appeal against a batsman even if you don't think he hit the ball, but it is not acceptable to appeal if the ball bounces before you catch it. Hard and fast rules exist in cricket values, despite the difference between the two situations being minor. Perhaps it is the doubt that a batsman may have hit the ball as opposed to the ball definitely bouncing.

The contest became increasingly dour with only three scoring shots in eight overs off Chappell and Walker. Meanwhile the Queen and the Duke of Edinburgh arrived half an hour early. They were met by VCA president Ray Steele and the official party moved to the VCA viewing area on the lower level of the Western stand, with the Queen's personal flag flying from the centre pole above the scoreboard. There was hope that the tradition of the sovereign's visit bringing a wicket would come true.

Cosier reflected on how much time he had spent at short leg where he had struggled to take a catch:

I had had a pretty crappy time at short leg where I hadn't quite got to a few catches. And was really down on myself for not making enough runs. I fielded there for most of match and the night before the final day I thought 'fuck this we've got a tour to England coming up and I'm probably out the window now, what can I do to redeem myself?

He had been watching the replay of the fourth day's play and saw himself fielding at short leg, going down on his left knee first before going forward, which restricted how far he could go forward with one leg on the ground. Cosier decided he would get in as close to the batsman as possible and put the weight on the balls of his feet as he leaned forward.

England were 3–346 when O'Keeffe returned to the attack His penultimate ball bounced and spun, enticing Randall forward. His bat pad edged to Cosier at short leg, who dived forward to take the catch and held the ball up to the crowd. Randall had batted for seven hours and scored 174 runs.

When Cosier held the ball to the crowds it was in response to the crowd at fine leg who had been sledging him for the past five days. At times the comments were vitriolic, along the lines of 'Cosier you are the worst cricketer in the world…you're a disgrace and couldn't get a game for Victoria and now you're back here.'

Jack Singleton compared Randall's batting to that of Peter May and Dennis Compton. Randall had an inglorious exit when he went through the wrong gate to the end of a special path leading to where the Queen and the Duke of Edinburgh were sitting. When he got to within a few metres of them he realised his mistake and bowed before making a quick retreat across the public seats!

In 2103 Randall reflected to the BBC:

I always get lost at the best of times but can you imagine walking off this ground where I had no idea how to get off. I went down the wrong exit (for the Queen). I thought, well

I've had a good day that could be for me.

The Australians had largely spent the hour before tea trying to dry up the runs, to give Lillee a rest and build pressure on England to have to chase the runs quickly. The last thing they wanted was to allow England to get into a position where they could cruise to a win.

During the tea break the players lined up in front of the Western stand to meet the Queen and the Duke. Her Majesty spent a few minutes talking with the bandaged McCosker. Lillee, though, took the attention when he asked her for an autograph. 'Can I have your autograph Ma'am?' asked Lillee, offering up a first-day cover envelope of the special issue of Centenary Test stamps already covered with signatures.

She declined and then later sent him a signed photo of the incident.

The Queen and the Duke were driven around the ground in an open Rolls Royce, even attracting an irreverent chant of 'Lizee, Lizee' from the patrons in Bay 13. It was not the first royal visit. George, Prince of Wales laid the foundation stone of the Melbourne Cricket Club's pavilion while serving on HMS Bacchante in Australian waters. The Queen had also attended ex-servicemen and school children's gatherings on the MCG while the Duke had opened the Olympic Games in 1956.

The match was set for a gripping final session with England needing 109 to win.

The game tilted back Australia's way not long after tea. The Queen was meeting the former Australian Prime Minister Sir Robert Menzies in the Long Room when O'Keeffe's wrong 'un was sufficiently deceptive for Greig to bat pad to Cosier at short leg. Greig was gone for 41 just when he looked like he might just help guide England to an unlikely win.

Cosier remembers the catch as 'an easy one':

> *The ball jammed between bat and pad, I took three steps but the ball was spinning like hell. The ball bounced out of my hands and I grabbed it again. It could have been the greatest fuck up of all time.*

A wave of relief came over Greg Chappell. 'We knew that once Greig was gone it would make it that much harder for England to win.'

The match was still in progress when the Queen and Duke left for the National Gallery of Victoria to unveil the $US380,000 Renoir painting 'The Guitarist'. The Queen noted a cricket reference in her speech:

> As Queen of Australia and the United Kingdom (long applause) I have no difficulty in enjoying this latest encounter in the 100 years battle between Australia and England for the unveiling of the Jubilee art exhibition.

It was midnight before the *Britannia* left Melbourne to head to South Australia for the next leg of her visit.

Knott continued on defiantly with some attacking strokes against Lillee that defied logic. Chris Old flashed outside off stump to edge to Chappell off Lillee. Lever was forced by O'Keeffe on to the back foot and was out lbw. After 84 minutes Alan Knott succumbed lbw to Lillee striking him in front on the left pad and Max O'Connell raised his finger. As the jubilant Australians walked from the field amid spectators who had run on the ground, Greg Chappell and Garry Cosier lifted Lillee onto their shoulders as a salute to the champion's performance. All three men looked exhausted.

The game was over with Australia 45 runs ahead. It was the exact same result as it had been 100 years before. Australia had won by just 45 runs to provide the perfect bookends for the first one hundred years of Test cricket.

Western Australian batsman Craig Serjeant who had been filing radio reports for a Perth radio station was one of the first to realise the result of the match was the same as it had been one hundred years before and he happily reported this back to his Perth audience.

Lillee had taken 5–139 off 34.4 overs. It was a remarkable effort from Lillee who looked completely drained of energy as he was grabbed by the crowd as a dozen or so policemen surrounded him.

England all out 417, Australia won by 45 runs, final day attendance, 31,392 to give a match figure of 248,260 and gate of $418,018.

DAY FIVE REFLECTIONS

And so it was all over.

The sports segment of *The Age* led with 'Lillee Foils Gallant Chase' where Peter McFarline wrote, 'Australia won the Centenary Test at 5:11pm yesterday by 45 runs—the same margin as in the first Test match at the same venue in 1977.'

Randall is pictured walking off, 'Derek 'the juggler' Randall, 174 runs to his name, quits the scene of his triumph.'

Also featured was a cartoon of two spectators walking from the MCG with the man saying to the woman, 'First time I haven't had to shout ''ave a go you mug'' at the Poms.'

The Australian Test touring side to England was named, 'Thomson in tour-team trial soon', as the article explains:

> *Thomson has been ordered to report for a medical examination on 4 April and to undergo a bowling trial in Sydney on 18 April. The selectors...were anxious to have him in the team following the withdrawal yesterday of Dennis Lillee for health and family reasons.*

Having played in the Centenary Test, Australia's all rounder Gary Gilmour found himself out of the squad of 17 for the tour of England.

As the April edition of *Cricketer* would rather cruelly observe, 'Almost overnight Gilmour had turned into a pumpkin...from the apparent "golden boy" of Australian cricket with his limitless natural ability into a nobody.'

Gilmour, a Packer signee would comment, 'Now I've got five rotten months to have the rest I needed for just a week during the season. The Achilles tendon trouble has been the reason why my bowling has gone to pot. I just couldn't stretch for fear of breaking down.'

The news of the Australian triumph was spread between adverts for Lukey mufflers 'anti-corrosive aluminium steel', Flemington's autumn carnival finale and Channel Nine News in 'living colour'. An interesting sideline is 'The Sheedy Story', an advert for Inside football, 'from the back streets of Prahran to become one of the toughest and most talented Tigers in modern football.' The shift to football season would be a seamless one.

All the talk after the match was about Derek Randall. Rated highly by the English players, the Australians knew little about him before the match. Randall's eccentricity, though, was obvious. His century was replete with a range of orthodox and non-orthodox strokes and even a new way of avoiding a bouncer—a text-book backward roll, before springing back up to a bewildered Dennis Lillee.

The Australians received Randall with degrees of bewilderment, annoyance and amusement. Any moves to unsettle him were met with cheerful banter in response, as Randall was a manic mix of movement and chatter. The Australians had never encountered anything or anyone like it.

Randall later said of his eccentricities, 'It was just natural for me. I'm a very outgoing character. I'm at my worst when I'm quiet. I like to be doing something or saying something.'

Part of the reason for Randall's success was the stability he felt batting early in his innings with Mike Brearley, who stressed to him the need to bat in 15-minute segments. 'You can't think about end products or winning the game you can only think about it in short periods and that's basically what we did.'

Greg Chappell noted:

> For a very complicated person his batting was quite uncomplicated, even when he was hit in the head he bounced back to his feet and doffed his cap to Dennis Lillee. There as an eccentricity about him that was both annoying and endearing.

Tony Greig, frustrated with Randall's inability to convert starts into scores, took Randall aside before the second innings. Greig said:

> I pushed him into a corner and told him the time had come for him to go out and make a big score otherwise people

would question him and his ability to kick on, otherwise he
may not be in the side for very long.

Dennis Lillee described Derek Randall's innings as:

...one of the all-time great digs...the guy threw caution to
the wind and attacked and gave it everything and played a
brilliant innings and got quite cheeky in it too. He was full
of beans, the great thing about it was the way he played the
game should be played. He went out and attacked from the
start.

It had been an amazing finish to a match that had initially threatened to
finish by day three.

In hindsight, Greg Chappell, who believes he only played on one or two
Test match wickets that were more challenging than the first morning of
the Centenary Test, thought the wicket was a day late in its preparation:

If we'd started on the second day then the team batting first
may have been a little inconvenienced for the first session
but after that it was a pretty good wicket. On the last day
it was still a very good batting wicket. In fact, England
probably should have won.

One of the highlights for the players was to meet with the Queen at tea
on the final day. With the match evenly poised the players remained on the
ground as their blazers were brought out to them. There was, though, an
unlikely gate crasher to festivities. As Greg Chappell observed:

As the official party came down the player's race I noticed
one of my friends (a Brisbane solicitor called Ian Harris)
at the end of it. 'What are you doing here?' I asked. He just
put his hand to this mouth as to stay quiet.

The interloper, who had his camera at hand, had somehow found a pause in the official party's line and jumped in the queue with no-one noticing. He managed to take some good photos but it was an incident you would hope wouldn't be repeated in this day and age.

For Chappell it was a funny incident to help lighten the mood. 'I was concerned that the Test was getting away from us but at a bit of levity at that time was fairly important.'

For Randall, hero status was granted. This eccentric Lancastrian had won over the hearts of the Australian cricket pubic, an affection that would continue throughout his career.

After the formalities Greg Chappell remembered the atmosphere in the dressing room straight after the match as being quietly subdued. As he sat with his feet up in the dressing room drinking a beer, the emotion he experienced was one of relief, 'We'd done what we'd hoped to do, I don't know if it dawned on us immediately that the result was the same as it was for the First Test.'

As Ray Bright sat in the dressing room mulling over what the previous five days had meant he thought Dennis Lillee was a little unlucky at missing out on the man of the match award: 'He bowled almost fifty overs and took 11 wickets for the match. He challenged the batsmen's stumps all the time. We were effectively a bowler down as Gary Gilmour was injured and only bowled nine overs for the match.'

Rod Marsh thought along similar lines as he marvelled at Lillee's performance, 'he tried every trick on the book that day; he bowled fast, he bowled cutters, swingers, slower balls, he bowled the whole lot.'

For Rick McCosker when the post-match euphoria started to sink in the Australian opener wasn't sure what to think. McCosker found it difficult. He had done a 'little bit' for the team but hadn't spent one moment in the field except for the sessions batting. He was simply admiring of the courage of Dennis Lillee to bowl through his back injury and finish with 11 wickets for the match: 'After the match it was quiet for a while and then it dawned upon us we'd won this fantastic Test match and the result was the same.'

When it was all over Ray Bright remembers a brief celebration involving a few long neck beers and then most of the players dispersing pretty early to head home.

After the match, Ian Davis was keeping mum about his meeting with Cornwell in the Hotel Windsor when Austin Robertson walked over gave him an envelope:

> *You get to keep these if we all agree on something. I got back to my hotel room and opened the envelope to find a cheque for eight grand. I thought, 'Shit! I just played my arse off for 50 bucks a day.'*

When a week later Davis had signed up and not mentioned the proposed deal to anyone, it was for a contract for $22,500 per year, plus bonuses, for three years.

Davis says while the money was a lot more than they were getting his signing wasn't about the money. 'Younger blokes like me and Hookesy just thought that if Ian Chappell says he wants us to be part of it then we would be a part of it. I didn't think twice about it or any of the ramifications.'

A number of players I have spoken to have echoed the same thought, that if Ian Chappell wanted them in they would be part of it. It gives some indication as to how significant a personality Chappell was when it came to the influence he had on younger players.

Close to 250,000 people had attended the match over five days. The bar in the MCG Long Room did a roaring trade. Bar manager Pat Kelly reported, 'We went through 16 barrels of beer each day of the match, and that's a record.'

For those decrying the commercialisation of the event they need only be reminded that it was a matter of 'everything old becoming new again'. The sponsorship of the Melbourne grocery firm of Spiers and Pond led to the first ever England team to Australia in 1862.

THE VOTING FOR THE MAN OF THE MATCH

Despite the overall admiration for his performance, there was some controversy surrounding the choice of England's Derek Randall as the man of the match. There were seven judges Peter McFarline from *The Age*, Rod Nicholson from *The Herald*, Alan Shiell from the Adelaide *News*, Alan McGilvray from the ABC, Henry Blofeld from the BBC, Peter Smith from the *Daily Mail* and Pat Gibson from the *Daily Express*.

Alan Shiell remembers having to vote well before the match had finished in order for Tony Syme, The Benson & Hedges representative, to collect the votes (by then Lillee had only taken three of his five second-innings wickets). Shiell and McGilvray voted for Marsh, while the remainder voted for Randall, arguing that if it hadn't been for Randall the match wouldn't have gone deep into the fifth day.

Once the match had ended, Shiell felt a sense of injustice and changed his vote to Lillee, believing that he was the match winner:

> *I went to the media area to see Tony Syme and Alan McGilvray was there too also wanting to change his vote to Lillee. It didn't matter as Randall had won all the other votes. Not long after I went into the Australian dressing room and saw Bob Parish and Ray Steele. Parish said to me 'I know who you voted for Alan.' It was if it was a nod of approval that I had voted for Lillee. Then suddenly they came up with a bowler of the match award to give to Dennis. It was some consolation as I know a number of the Australian players were disappointed that Dennis had missed out on the man of the match award.*

In the presentation ceremony VCA President Ray Steel handed Lillee a silver cup that was a replica of the 1877 trophy awarded by *The Australasian* to the best colonial bowler.

Lillee, looking exhausted, walked up to the podium to accept the award from ACB's Treasurer Ray Steele. 'I'd just like to say it was a great test it couldn't have been more fitting for a centenary and I'm just glad we won it.'

Derek Randall's man-of-the-match award, saw him take home a cheque for $1500 and a gold medallion. The Australians smiled when they heard Randall's acceptance speech which included thanking Lillee for 'the bump on the head'.

CHAPTER XX

Post-Centenary Test

Reverberations

When it was all over most involved were exhausted. It had been a week of keenly fought cricket as well as cricket functions every night of the match.

Frank Tyson, in summing up the match for a television audience, described it as 'a combination of a thrilling match, a royal pageant and a stroll down memory lane…this has been the Olympic games of cricket.'

McCosker started the long road to recovery after his injury, which affected him physically but also mentally. After the match he returned to Sydney to have another X-ray, with the specialist informing McCosker that his jaw had to be re broken and wired up. This meant another week in hospital and six weeks of drinking and eating out of a straw sampling his wife's tomato soup and gravy, meat and vegetables all packaged up into a liquid. It also meant limited exercise. It was hardly the ideal preparation for an arduous tour of England

For Derek Randall the 1977 Centenary Test became the milestone of his career, no matter how many highs and lows he experienced throughout his cricket career he would always be remembered for scoring 174. When we look at history it is easy to assume that things were always going to happen the way they did. We forget that leading into the Centenary Test Randall was a four-Test novice, undecided even if he would play in the match itself.

In fact, England's new number four batsman had felt very nervous leading into the Centenary Test. The sense of occasion was exciting but adding to those jangling nerves. He sat at a dinner table before the start of the match opposite Don Bradman, Ray Lindwall and Keith Miller. Next to him either side were two Nottingham legends, Harold Larwood and Bill Voce:

> *When Harold went to the toilet I went with him just so I didn't miss a story. I remember it as the most wonderful evening of my life and that's what made it so special, you've got all the history of these great players and the battles between the two sides. Larwood even told me how he was sponsored by Home Ales who had sent out beer for him to have with his breakfast every morning.*

For Derek Randall a hero status was granted. This eccentric Lancastrian had won over the hearts of the Australian cricket pubic, an affection that would continue throughout his career.

When Gary Cosier returned to Adelaide after the match he gave his cricket gear away to his brother in Melbourne. He didn't think he'd be needing it for a while. Cosier was adamant that his two soft dismissals in the match would see him dropped from the side to tour England. He was shocked that some suggested that the match had been fixed to ensure that the result would be the same as the first Test in 1877:

> *Some people came up to me and said that they thought the match was fixed, what were the odds, they asked, that the match result would be exactly the same? And I thought how the hell; could you fix a cricket game, surely you can't fix a game of cricket. Little did I know how things would change.*

Tony Greig was adamant that despite meeting up with Barry Richards, who was spending the English off season playing and coaching in Perth, at the WACA before the tour match, he knew nothing about the plans for World Series Cricket.

Greig says that when the English players flew home after the Centenary Test he stayed behind to look up a few businesses contacts and keep an appointment with Kerry Packer although he was at pains to point out:

> *I had made the appointment with Mr Packer and I had made it purely to sound him out on the possibility of earning some money by broadcasting on his television network. Television commentating was something that appealed to me and Packer was one of the big names in the business.*

It was at this meeting at Packer's Bellevue Hill home in Sydney that Packer made what Greig described as 'the most extraordinary counter-proposal I have ever heard'—sign up for World Series Cricket, recruit overseas players and be guaranteed a job for life with Channel Nine.

The fact that a number of Australian players were signed during the Centenary Test had no bearing on Greg Chappell's memory of the match. Chappell saw the encounter as one of the best Test matches he played in and certainly one of the most draining because of all the pageantry, the challenge of the match itself and the fact that it was decided in the last hour of the final day and could have gone either way. 'I remember after the match putting my feet up in the dressing room, having a beer and savouring the moment of winning what was always going to be something that would stand out from other Tests.'

When the WSC story broke after Tony Greig's infamous party at Sussex in May 1977, the Australian captain, Greg Chappell, was still unaware as to how many players had signed. Until then it had been business as usual for the Australian tourists:

> *The Australian Cricket Board reacted as only the Board can and started a campaign of divide and conquer*

particularly focusing on younger players like David
Hookes and Ian Davis. The Board tried to undermine
their confidence which wasn't hard to do as no-one really
knew what was going on, so it was even more confusing
for the younger players.

Greg Chappell believes that Kerry Packer's takeover of cricket was something that was always going to happen. He thought that although they had a commercially successful series, Test cricket was in danger of losing its gloss. It needed renewal and he doesn't know if it would have happened under the conservative leadership that was around. It needed a shake-up:

> *It would be interesting to know where the game would have*
> *got to. Although cricket was still healthy there would have*
> *been more pressure on the Boards at the time. It would have*
> *been much harder to make changes if the game had started to*
> *decline, the time was right. It took someone who understood*
> *the game and the impact of colour TV to carry it off.*

No clearer example of the invisible divide between the players and the Australian Cricket Board was illustrated by how little contact the Australian captain Greg Chappell had with Sir Donald Bradman at the match. Although Bradman was still heavily involved in the game he appeared to keep at arm's length from the players. 'I saw more of the Queen than I did Bradman during the Test', said Chappell.

Ray Bright missed most of the official functions. He didn't stay with the rest of the side at Melbourne's Hilton hotel but rather looked forward each night to sitting down with his parents at the Bright family home, eating whatever his mum had cooked up. At the time it was common policy for Test players competing in home Tests to stay at their own house. He did however enjoy the occasional conversation with the likes of Sam Loxton, Neil Harvey and Alec Bedser at the ground.

Rick McCosker spent a large portion of the Centenary Test listening to the match from his hospital bed on radio. McCosker who was employed in a bank in Sydney had been asked to sign up for WSC but decided not to make the decision until after the Centenary Test:

> *I was visited by Austin Robertson and John Cornell and knew that if they were asking me then they were asking all the other guys. I knew that I wouldn't be the first one asked. It was a big decision to make but we were the number one team in the world but basically not receiving much of the proceeds. There were other issues as well—the fact we started playing more and more cricket and the guys were trying to balance more cricket, minor income payments and trying to work as well and a lot of us were at the stage were we had young families.*

McCosker lost his job at the bank when it became aware that he had signed for WSC. He was asked to choose between the two.

Australia's medium-paced all-rounder Max Walker described the Centenary as 'one of the best Test matches I ever played in'. 'It was like a soap opera with a lot going on behind the scenes with players being signed up by Kerry Packer.'

One vivid memory is of Doug Walters trying to make Rick McCosker, who had his jaw all wired up, laugh:

> *Walters was quick to quip after we found out that the result was the same as one hundred years before 'Look in all this time the Poms haven't got any better…100 years later the result is still the same!'*

For Walters it proved to be the most memorable match he played in and one where the relationship between the players was as friendly as with any game he played in. 'I played in closer Test matches but this was the most memorable because of the whole aura of the event.'

Veteran journalist Peter McFarline praised Tony Greig's open press policy. 'You can talk as much as you like to any of the players at any time', Greig told Australian reporters. A policy, McFarline noted, that has not always been the case. It's also worth noting that Brearley and Randall turned down talks with cricket writers unless they were paid.

AUSTRALIA'S ASHES TOUR OF ENGLAND,

1977

Australia's tour of England in 1977 was in trouble before it began. Unknown to cricket officials was the fact that 13 of the 17 had already signed a contract with Kerry Packer to play a series of matches for television the following season.

When news of the signings broke on 9 May in Sussex in England, it was like a cloudburst on a fine summer's day. Not only were the Australian signees uncertain of their future but the future of the game itself was unknown. Reporters Alan Shiell and Peter McFarline broke the story. Ian Davis thought it was David Hookes who had let the cat out of the bag, thinking Hookes must have had a few beers and let it slip to his fellow South Australian, Alan Shiell. Shiell has never revealed the source.

UK newspapers were against Packer and his mission while the Australian papers reacted as if those involved were traitors. Peter McFarline with the Melbourne *Age* described Packer as such: 'He not only looked like a hammerhead shark but acted like one.'

The UK's *Daily Mail* provided a nautical theme with a front page headline that screamed, 'World's Top Cricketers Turn Pirate'.

Once the news of the signings occurred the Australian cricket board immediately decided to place pressure on the younger players of the Australian side.

Ian Davis knew the Chair of the ACB well from his time playing at Northern Districts. When Australia played at Trent Bridge in June Tim Caldwell asked Davis to meet him in the Notts office after play. He told Davis that he thought it was sad that Davis had decided to sign telling him he'd 'blown his Test career' and that one day he could have been captain of Australia:

> *He told me that it was okay for the other blokes as they were old…but he said we care about the young fellahs who are throwing away their careers…he then asked me if I would consider breaking my contract.*

'Why don't you go away and have a think about it?' Caldwell rang Davis the next day and asked how he was feeling. Davis replied 'I'm feeling a bit ordinary…I'm starting to think that I made the wrong decision…I jumped on because I was one of the boys.' Caldwell assured Davis that the Board would help him break his contract, pay their legal costs and support them.

The Board had also approached David Hookes and Mick Malone.

A story appeared in the media that a number of Packer signees were about to break ranks. Davis believes Caldwell leaked the story. 'A week later Rod Marsh said to me that Kerry Packer was on his way over.'

A few days later Kerry Packer arrived in London to test them out. The 13 players were summoned to meet him at the Dorchester Hotel. Packer lined them all up and asked for confirmation that they were committed to the contracts.

Packer was clear in what he had to say. He had heard that some of the players wanted to break their contract with WSC. If they were to proceed along that path he informed the players, then he would take them to court to recover damages. That was after he'd told them in a forceful tone 'anyone who breaks their contract with me would "lose everything".'

Davis, found himself sinking further and further down in his seat and remembered Packer threatening to 'take your house, your car…everything you've got'. Packer then directed his attention to Davis. 'I've given you the chance of a lifetime and you're going to break a contract with me...no-one breaks a contract with me.'

Davis later called Caldwell to inform him he wasn't breaking his contract. He also felt the cold shoulder from some senior team-mates at his hesitation. Davis described the 1977 tour as 'a disaster'.

Packer, had well-respected former Australian captain and broadcaster Richie Benaud in his corner. Benaud had an outstanding understanding of the game that was brought to the viewers with his dry style and wry, observant wit. Benaud, who was on a consultancy fee of $30,000, advising Packer on how to attempt negotiations with the ACB and on setting up WSC, also had plenty of journalism and public relations experience. Benaud was able to warn Packer as to how the Australian and English Cricket Boards and various media outlets would react. 'As this (WSC) is a Channel 9 exclusive production, there will be resistance from other media...you shouldn't think that there won't be some sniping from all sections of the media.'

Bradman attacked the concept and said that Packer's main motivation was to gain the TV rights to Test cricket in Australia. Bradman refused to answer Benaud's calls, signalling the start of a several years' rift, during which they would not speak.

Packer's plans had already changed the thinking of English cricket authorities when it came to pay. Mike Selvey recalls being paid 210 pounds a test in 1976 and 2,400 pounds for a four-month tour of India, Sri Lanka and Australia. By the time the 1977 Ashes series rolled around players were paid 1000 pounds per test match. In 12 months' payment for playing in a test match had increased by a factor of five.

The ACB wanted little to do with the Australian captain, Greg Chappell. While the team manager, Len Maddocks, gave Chappell a dressing down, the Board felt that Chappell had misled it as he had signed to represent the Board and WSC, but Chappell was not in breach of any contract as he intended to, and did, fulfil his obligations as Test captain until September and then resigned after the 1977 Ashes tour.

One of the signees was Rick McCosker, whose tour got off to a delayed start. Having had surgery to fix his broken jaw it was arranged that he would leave a week after the touring party. That turned to two weeks when an air-traffic controller strike left McCosker stranded at Sydney Airport. When he finally arrived in England, he found cold, wet English summer and green wickets making it difficult for batting, even harder given McCosker's inability to practise before he left.

For McCosker, the main lure of WSC was to play with and against the best in the world 'The money was part of it but I wanted to be part of World Series Cricket…I wasn't interested in the contracts the others had.' McCosker, who struggled to find form, was less distracted by WSC more so by the need to find form quickly.

Australian left-arm orthodox spinner Ray Bright was first approached by Kerry Packer in April of 1977, once the celebrations of the Centenary Test had died down. Austin Robertson came calling and then, after a few probing questions, Ian Chappell contacted Bright with assurance that he was involved and that the bloke running the show, Kerry Packer, was the real deal. Bright appreciated Chappell's honesty when he asked whether it might mean the end of his Test career. 'Quite possibly', he replied.

It didn't matter. He signed for slightly less than the standard $25,000 a year contract. Even though he was just 22, Bright wanted to play among and against the best cricketers in the world. When Bright boarded the plane to England for the 1977 tour he still didn't know who had signed.

Fragmented, was how Ray Bright described the Australian side during the 1977 tour. He made his Test debut during the Second Test at Manchester. The Australians heard the pitch was proving spin friendly and Bright got the call up to bowl in tandem with Kerry O'Keeffe. Bright took three first-innings wickets but Australia was trumped by nine wickets. Bright also suffered the ignominy of being dismissed for a second innings duck, caught and bowled by spinning opponent Derek Underwood.

A highlight of the match for Bright was his first innings dismissal of the man who he had watched score a magnificent 174 in the second innings of the Centenary Test. He trapped Randall lbw for 79 as England scored a first innings total of 437. So disappointing was the tour for Bright and his team-mates he things it still gnaws away at them. 'The tour still eats away at a lot of players who thought they should have done better.'

Test cricket was another experience for Bright who was leaning that it could be a difficult and frustrating game to play. 'I soon found out that you could bowl well and not necessarily take wickets.'

One relationship that did improve on the 1977 tour was that between Kerry O'Keeffe and David Hookes. O'Keeffe's early impressions of Hookes were tainted when they had first met a few seasons before. Hookes told O'Keeffe he thought that he was a good bowler, before adding, 'for a club player'.

One of their common interests on the England tour was the England tennis player, Sue Barker, who they had met at Wimbledon that year. Both had tried to capture her attention. When O'Keeffe found out that Hookes scored a date with the attractive, blonde-haired Barker, O'Keeffe asked whether she sent him her love. 'Regards', was the answer from Hookes, 'She sends her regards'.

Rick McCosker remembers a connection with his spiritual self during the 1977 tour, one where he occasionally was able to sneak away and attend a church service:

> *I always had a faith while I was playing. But it wasn't at the forefront partly because I didn't have a lot of opportunities when I was travelling partly because it wasn't cool at that stage to be up front about being a church goer...because I didn't want to be found out we travelled a lot and played a lot on Sundays so there weren't many opportunities. It wasn't as big a part of my life as it has become but I always felt better when I could get to church.*

There was a point during the 1977 tour when McCosker was feeling down and depressed and he knew he was in danger of being dropped from the Australian side. The team were in Manchester before heading to Trent

Bridge in Nottingham for the next Test. Around the corner from the team hotel was the cathedral of Manchester, where McCosker paid a visit while the other players went off to the golf course.

At the end of the mass, just as McCosker was leaving the priest said, 'This morning we have an Australian cricketer with us. He's been down for a while and we pray for peace for him and that he will have faith in the talent he has.' McCosker was gobsmacked. 'I walked from the cathedral to the hotel and felt a completely different person and later made a comment to Rod Marsh that I was going to score a century.' He hit 51 in the first innings before scoring 107 in the second. McCosker's good form, sadly, didn't see a turnaround in Australia's performance as they lost 3–0.

The ACB and the English TCCB were in agreeance that they had to find a way to stop Packer. They saw Test cricket was in jeopardy, as was their survival as ruling bodies.

After the tour the British media continued its vilification of Packer. Back in Australia WSC-signed players were snubbed at club level. Ian Chappell was fired as North Melbourne's captain and Max Walker couldn't get picked for The Melbourne Cricket Club. Lesser lights such as Ray Bright and Ray Robinson had to turn out on suburban grounds to get a game of cricket.

The Board tried to stop WSC from using training facilities. The MCG and SCG weren't available for its use. Even the International Cricket Conference, in conjunction with the TCCB, rewrote the rules to prevent cricketers from playing WSC.

The ICC, which comprised representatives of Australia, India, New Zealand, Pakistan and the West Indies, announced that anyone contracted to Packer, as of 1 October, would be ineligible to play Test matches without the express consent of the Conference. Packer, though, was across the manipulations, directing his lawyers to seek an injunction and damages in a London High Court action against the ICC and the TCCB. The Court found their action was an unreasonable restraint of trade. Packer's group was awarded costs of $350,000 and the contracted cricketers were free to play.

The Cricket War would take its toll. From 1977–78 through to the reconciliation two years later there were two national Australian cricket teams existing, seemingly, in parallel universes: the glamorous rock-star realm of World Series Cricket; and the harsh reality of traditional test cricket, suddenly depicted as stodgy and obsolete but nevertheless hard fought, by young, poorly-paid men who represented their country in a time honoured contest.

Australian cricket would be torn apart with many friendships lost. It would take two years for the reconciliation and even then there remained a sense of uncertainty between the warring parties. Cricket had been thrust into the modern world of sport and many years would pass before a sense of the normality that was usually associated with the Australian cricket brand returned. But even when it did, the game was not the same.

Although it only crossed two Australian summers many friendships were lost and the bitterness remained for years after. Some players would become defined by whether they were WSC or Establishment player. Rod Marsh and Dennis Lillee would be immediately associated with the break-away Packer brand and lose leadership opportunities that may well have come their way. Marsh was perhaps the worst affected, as a player who would have made an outstanding captain of Australia but was never given the opportunity. In fact, had he been given the leadership role it is more than likely he would have played beyond the 1983–84 season, when the triumvirate of Marsh, Lillee and Greg Chappell retired from Test cricket after that summer's final test against Pakistan.

CHAPTER XXVII

1980—A CENTENARY TOO FAR

It was just three years later that the MCC organised their own Centenary Test to mark the first time a Test was played on English soil. Although the first was played at the Oval, its centenary was played at what was considered the home of cricket, Lord's, in the hope of accommodating larger crowds. But for this occasion the champagne was flat after the excitement of the extraordinary Centenary Test of 1977. Just as the 1977 Centenary Test was memorable for all the right reasons, sadly the 1980 match would prove to be a match shrouded in controversy and ruined by poor weather.

The England team for the encounter was, Ian Botham (captain), David Bairstow, Geoffrey Boycott, Graham Gooch, Charles Athey, David Gower, Mike Gatting, Peter Willey, John Emburey, Chris Old and Mike Hendrick.

The Australian team was Greg Chappell (captain), Rod Marsh, Graeme Wood, Bruce Laird, Kim Hughes, Allan Border, Len Pascoe, Dennis Lillee, Ray Bright, Ashley Mallett and Graham Yallop.

There were some highlights, notably, two superb innings by Kim Hughes. In fact, so good was Hughes' performance in the Centenary Test at Lord's, he was named a Wisden Cricketer of the Year for a single performance, (the others were Robin Jackman, Allan Lamb, Clive Rice and Vincent van der Bijl). Hughes' performance went against his tour form, in which he struggled. Apart from scores of an undefeated 73 and 98 in the one-day internationals, Hughes' scores against the counties read 0, 4 not out, 16, 5, 0 and 9. Hughes had shown signs, though, that the unconventional had merit. Against Hampshire he had struck the winning runs with a one-handed square-cut off Mark Nicholas and performed two left-arm sweeps in the one-day international at Edgbaston.

Ray Bright was one of the players who took part in the 1977 Centenary Test as well as the 1980 match at Lord's. He says it lacked the great aura of the Melbourne match. That may be because the MCG held a special place in Bright's memory but also because the game was so rain-affected and petered out to a draw.

While the match was held only three years after the Melbourne test, it may as well have been a lifetime. Perhaps the cricketing gods didn't approve of the match being played at Lord's, the home of cricket, rather than where the 1880 contest had been held at the Oval.

Percy Fender, at the age of 88, made it into the stands as did Stork Hendry, three years his junior and a survivor of the famous 1921 team of Warwick Armstrong. The Q Stand, now the Allen stand, was reserved throughout for the legends of yesteryear.

The rain-soaked match has faded into oblivion rather than continued to shine as its Australian counterpart has all these years later. And how the fortunes of those who took part changed.

Australian batsman Kim Hughes, who lit up the leaden skies over London with two masterpieces of 117 and an undefeated 84 has been all but forgotten in cricketing folklore when compared with the feats of Derek Randall and Dennis Lillee in 1977.

There were more than ten hours of the match lost due to rain, although an extra hour of play was added to the final two days (only 75 minutes were possible on the second day). It was also a match marred by an unsavoury incident. When the umpires returned from the fifth inspection of the pitch, umpire Constant was assaulted by angry MCC members in the front of the Long Room.

Hughes became the third batsman to bat on all five days of a Test after ML Jaisimha and G Boycott. Hughes took 346 minutes and faced 308 balls in scoring a match aggregate of 201 containing five sixes and 25 fours.

Australia batted first and, with the help of Wood's 112 and Hughes' 117, made 385.

Despite Hughes' struggles in the lead up matches *The Guardian's* cricket writer Paul Fitzpatrick presciently described Hughes in his preview of the match:

> *I would suggest Hughes, if not the embodiment of Trumper, is at least a reminder of the great man. He had Trumper's clear gaze and good looks and a nature that one has yet to hear criticised: he has style.*

Hughes' biographer Chris Ryan also evoked memories of Trumper in his book *Golden Boy: Kim Hughes and the Bad Old Days of Australian Cricket:*

> *Now Old was Galumphing in. Right line. Short of a length. Dangerous ball. Kim took one small step forward, then one large skip, bat raising behind him. His back foot pivoted. A puff of dust stirred. Freeze framed, it was like a full colour replica of George Bedlam's photo of Trumper stepping out to drive the ball. The ball nearly burst. The cameras lost it. Umpire Dickie Bird swivelled round. Non-striker Greg Chappell clapped his bat. Mike Gatting on the leg side laughed. Voices cracked in the ABC commentary box.*

John Woodcock, writing in *The Times,* was appreciative that the timing of the Test match meant schoolchildren could watch Hughes in action to study his orthodox technique.

Despite the rain, the match provided Hughes' golden hour. A quick glance at YouTube provides some of the highlights of Hughes' knocks. When Hughes struck Old for a six, an amusing interchange occurred between the commentators, the ABC's Norman May and cricketing great

Keith Miller. 'Down the ground again', said May, 'What a shot...We'll nearly catch that. A magnificent hit. That almost finished in our broadcast box. Keith have you ever seen a bigger hit at Lord's than that one?'

In what was a lucky break for May to have Miller on air with him at the time, Miller replied, 'Well I hit a couple up there myself Norman oddly enough. But not many have. That is one of the biggest hits I've seen for many, many a year. On top of the balcony.' The ball had travelled around 125 metres. Almost clearing the roof of the Member stand.

Hughes almost completed a feat achieved just once before, by Albert Trott in 1899.

Greg Chappell declared towards the end of the third day. The day had promised much with a dry night raising hopes of an on-time start, but a two-hour downpour in the morning washed away much of the optimism. What angered the crowd were the constant pitch inspections carried out by the umpires Dickie Bird and David Constant and the captains Greg Chappell and Ian Botham. Under clear skies and bright sunshine, a full house, the crowd watched the officials gesticulating and not much more. In the Test Match Special box, John Arlott observed, 'I do wish that everybody could be entertained by the great dramatic presentation of Dickie Bird worrying about to have play or not.'

England responded with 205. Boycott's 62 and Gower's 45, the stand outs for England. Botham scored a duck (his pair in 1981 would take Botham to three ducks in a row versus Australia at Lord's). Pascoe's best bowling for Australia (5–59) included a spell of five–10 in 32 balls.

Australia declared at 4–189 when Kim Hughes was lbw to Botham for 84. Needing 370 runs to win in 350 minutes England scored 3–244. Boycott scored an undefeated 128 and passed the 7000 run Test mark, following in the footsteps of Wally Hammond, Colin Cowdrey and Garry Sobers. The highlight of the match was the acknowledgement of the end of the wonderful commentary career of John Arlott after 35 years.

On the Saturday of the match, with a big crowd in when the sun was shining, there was still no play:

> *What I hate is this sun blazing down and people are getting none...I think they (the crowd) are not quite content and patient and they have every right to be. What they are facing is the worse type of bureaucracy which is doing things by the letter of the law instead of the spirit of the law. What they want is some cricket even if they are told the fieldsman's not to go in to the mud, Surely these people playing in a historic match celebrating 100 years of test cricket with a Saturday crowd out there will say we'll go out there even if we do slip.*

Many would have agreed with Arlott's typical straight-talking sentiments. His last piece of commentary was as crisp and businesslike:

> *Boycott pushed this away between silly point and slip... picked up by Mallett at short third man...the end of the over...nine runs off the over—28 Boycott, 15 Gower, 69 for 2—and after Trevor Bailey it will be Christopher Martin Jenkins.*

A standing reception echoed around the ground for several minutes as the players waited for the match to resume.

The match had ended in a tame draw. As cricket historian Warwick Franks put it, despite the rain it could have been different but for 'a lack of imaginative purpose from English captain Ian Botham and the obduracy of Geoff Boycott.'

While the game was a huge disappointment, the attendance, the welcoming parties and the dinners were all very successful. Cornhill Insurance even rented a London theatre for a night of ceremony.

After the bonhomie and cricketing success of the 1977 perhaps cricket authorities were too optimistic in scheduling a second Centenary Test. The rain had spoiled what could have been a wonderful event, but maybe also something else had changed. The relative innocence of the game had disappeared because some of the animosity remained after the Packer World Series Cricket. Some friendships were still strained so much they would never return to what they had been, others were lost for good. WSC had proven to be a pivotal yet painful period in the game's modern history. As Mike Coward wrote:

> *Cricket became a game bitterly divided. Resentment and suspicion ran deep and accusation and recrimination became the default position of the protagonists. As new allegiances were forged old bonds were broken and friendships shattered. Sir Donald Bradman and Richie Benaud, OBE, giants of the game whose vision and energy had famously given the kiss-of-life to moribund Test cricket 17 years earlier, did not speak for two years. They resented being compelled to direct their attention and affection to one of two Australian teams. Where should their loyalties lie: with those who upheld the honour and rich traditions of the fabled, 'baggy green' cap or the admired and seemingly opportunistic rebels who were hell bent on propelling the game into new and unfamiliar territory?*

Cricket had changed and would never be able to replicate the deeds of 1977 again.

CHAPTER

WHAT FOLLOWED FOR THE PLAYERS?

THE AUSTRALIAN PLAYERS

Greg Chappell was an important presence in World Series Cricket lending credibility and good form during the two-year period of the competition.

He made an eight-hour 174 in a Supertest at Gloucester Park in Perth in January 1978 following it with 246 at VFL Park in Melbourne. A year later he scored three centuries in successive Supertests. In 1979–80 he regained the Australian captaincy and was made an Australian selector. In the 1980 tour of Pakistan he made his highest test score of 235 in seven-and-a-half hours at Faisalabad. In 1980–81 he scored another double century (204) this time against India but the season was dominated by the underarm incident against New Zealand, where he ordered his brother Trevor to bowl the final ball underarm to ensure the win.

Chappell chose not to tour England on Australia's ill-fated tour of 1981 and returned with a fluent 201 in 1981–82 against Pakistan in Brisbane. A horror run followed. From mid December to late January he scored eight ducks in 15 successive innings in both Test and one-day internationals. He handed the leadership back to Kim Hughes when he was unavailable to tour Pakistan in 1982–83. In his final season of Test cricket Chappell scored 954 runs at 53, closing his test career as it had begun with a quality century (182) that took him past Bradman's test aggregate of 6996 runs. After retiring, he was a member of the ACB from 1984 until 1988, citing frustration with the archaic nature of the Australian cricket administration.

He went into coaching spending some time with South Australia and working as a consultant at Pakistan. He also worked as a commentator for the ABC and later Channel Nine. In May 2005 he was appointed coach of the Indian national cricket team on a two-year term—a period that ended with a falling out with the captain Sourav Gangully. He returned as an Australian selector for 2010–2011.

One of Chappell's closet cricketing allies, Rod Marsh, would bow out of test cricket in the same match against Pakistan in 1983–84—as, indeed, would fellow ally Dennis Lillee.

Marsh, who performed so brilliantly in the Centenary Test, was an astute, ambitious and highly credentialed leader who deserved his time at the top of Australian cricket. The chance for leadership was the main reason he initially hesitated when it came to joining up for WSC. Marsh later wrote:

> *If I had continued to play established cricket I would have been in line for the captaincy...I was the only bloke left with any test experience at all. I knew that all the other guys had signed and that I wouldn't be happy playing at a lower level than that which I was capable so I joined up.*

Had he stayed with the establishment he would surely have been a shoo-in to be captain. When the reconciliation arrived he was never given the Australian test captaincy. Until 1983–84 Marsh played 96 Tests and amassed 355 dismissals. Marsh's combination with Lillee produced a record 95 dismissals, 'c Marsh b Lillee'. He had a prolonged stint as coach of the Australian Cricket Academy where players of the ilk of Ricky Ponting and Glenn McGrath were unearthed. Marsh accepted the director's role of England's National Academy and later was appointed an England selector

Doug Walters was the most popular Australian cricketer of his generation. The 1977 tour of England marked his fourth tour where he hadn't scored a test century. A crooked backlift and tendency to play across the line had made him more vulnerable outside off stump. Walters' time with WSC involved few major matches and his international career appeared to be over with the reconciliation of 1979. He regained his Test place in 1980–81, scoring 107 against New Zealand in Melbourne and scoring 78 and an undefeated 18 in his final Test against India in Melbourne. He retired from Test cricket when he failed to make the Australian touring side to England in 1981.

Walters had the uncanny ability to turn a match with a session's batting or through an unexpected wicket with his slow–medium pacers. His two innings of the Centenary Test, where he failed dismally in the first innings yet came back with a solid dependable knock of 66 just when it was very much needed, reflect the frustrations and successes of his career.

During World Series Cricket, Ian Davis played five Supertests for Australia. His first match was against the West Indies in Melbourne in early December 1977, his last against the West Indies, also in Melbourne, in January 1979. His top score of 84 came against the World XI in Melbourne in February 1978.

Davis, however, came to regret his decision to play WSC:

> *If I had my time again would I have signed? Probably not. If I hadn't signed I would have probably played more Test cricket...I was 23 and impressionable and made the decision based on the fact that everyone else was doing it...but at the end of the day I'm proud of being part of it because it changed the whole cricket world.*

After the reconciliation Davis found it hard to get back in the New South Wales side and admits he became bitter:

> *From the moment I came back to the fold I had an uneasy feeling. If I had my chance again I would have just put my head down and not worried about all the crap that went on and just played the game.*

He scored a century against a Tasmanian side featuring New Zealand bowler Richard Hadlee (133) and found himself dropped for the next game (Border and Toohey returned from Test duties).

Davis continued to score runs with his district club, Balmain, even breaking Archie Jackson's record for most runs in a season. Davis' criticism of the New South Wales selectors did little to help his cause. 'At the end of the day I suppose I had a chip on my shoulder and felt many of the players that went to World Series Cricket were victimised because of their decision.'

He believes disruption of his career had a telling effect. 'I would have liked to have done better and think I probably would have if it wasn't so disrupted.' Davis' career represents the classic underachiever role. Picked too early and then interrupted by WSC just as he was finding his feet at Test level.

Davis later became general manager of Dunlop Slazenger before becoming a consultant for Spartan (the bats that Michael Clarke, MS Dhoni and Chris Gayle use), getting remarried and living on a golf course at Macquarie Links.

One of Gary Cosier's abiding memories of the Centenary Test was Rick McCosker's injury. Cosier was at the other end when McCosker was hit on the side of the cheek by Bob Willis. He had also been at the other end when Peter Toohey was hit by Andy Roberts in the West Indies in 1978. While Toohey's blow had been a hard knock, McCosker's had been a dull thud in the cheekbone, a sound that Cosier has not forgotten. In the light of Phil Hughes' death in November of 2014, Cosier remembers these incidents and one where he was struck by New South Wales speedster Len Pascoe: 'I was hit smack bang in the middle of my eyes at Adelaide Oval and didn't feel a thing. I was just lucky.'

For Cosier, the Centenary Test was a great disappointment, falling to the same stroke in each innings—the hook shot—for just 14 runs. 'I don't think I put enough thought into it. I don't think it was the occasion that got to me.' Cosier, though, was dealing with a deeply personal matter at the time:

When I returned from the New Zealand tour my wife had left me and I arrived at our four-bedroom house and there was just a camp stretcher, a can of beans, a can opener and a spoon. I stayed there for three or four days wondering what was going on and that was my preparation for the Centenary Test but I can't really remember my thought patterns at the time. It wasn't perfect but I'm not sure what part that played in it all. It came as a shock, I didn't know she was going to leave me. We were both young.

Although he doesn't say it, I get the sense that Cosier is a little miffed at the way that he was portrayed in the TV miniseries *Howzat! Kerry Packer's War* about World Series Cricket. In the TV series there is a scene where Rod Marsh asks, 'Do you want a beer?' Cosier replied yes, only for Marsh to tell him 'They're over there.'

'That didn't happen', says Cosier. 'There was never any sense of that stuff in the dressing room that indicated that something else was going on.'

Gary Cosier's fortunes as a test batsman are sharply divided on either side of the cricket war. Before Kerry Packer's intervention, Cosier had played nine tests and was averaging in the forties. After the establishment series against India, the West Indies and England his average had been curtailed to just 28. Cosier returned to Victoria from Queensland in 1980–81, failing in two state appearances and disappearing from the first-class scene. He did, however, win the Jack Ryder Medal that season and played on until 1986–87. He was also a Victorian selector in 1987–88 and 1988–89. For a while Cosier owned some indoor cricket centres and worked for a rent-a-car company. In the early 1980s Cosier was offered a position with International Management Group in Jakarta that started an international career. He spent 17 years working in places like Tangier and Morocco in northern Africa, where he ran golf properties, and he later became the CEO of Queensland's largest private golf club, Indooroopilly.

When WSC ended, Gary Gilmour returned to his native Newcastle to play for Belmont and appeared only twice more for New South Wales.

Gary Gilmour's last Test was the 1977 Centenary Test. Having bowled only nine overs and gone wicketless in the match, he was dropped from the touring side to England in 1977. He remembers the heckles from the crowds for being too fat and lazy, enjoyed his time playing World Series cricket but later wondered about the wisdom of the decision. He later told the ABC's Frank Crook:

> I quite enjoyed my two years but I wonder in hindsight if it was the best decision I've ever made. If I hadn't signed for WSC and kept playing for the Board would I have played longer in the game? I would have been on a lot stronger footing when the reconciliation occurred.

Gilmour was one, though, with few regrets, who played the game for the enjoyment.

> I played cricket with the attitude that I was out there to enjoy it. I liked to attack and as a batsman I took a lot of risks. I was of the opinion that if you are not enjoying what you are doing, why pursue it any further?

He died at the age of 62 in 2014 after battling health problems including the need for a liver transplant nine years earlier.

David Hookes provided one of the defining moments of World Series Cricket when he was struck by an Andy Roberts bouncer during a WSC Supertest. At one stage Hookes sought the help of a hypnotherapist to try and get the image of the ball out of his head. The moment was defining as it would later affect Hookes as a player, forever spooked by bouncers, but it also provided validity to what WSC represented. Despite being called derogatory names such as pyjama or circus cricket, the ball that broke Hookes' jaw proved the matches weren't exhibition matches but fiercely-fought contests between the best players in the world.

David Hookes, whose Test career, after such a promising start, spluttered along for close to a decade, ended up playing just 23 Tests. His one test century was against Sri Lanka at Kandy during the 1982–83 season, finishing with a test average of 34.3. His time in the WSC spotlight proved lucrative for a short period but Test success after reconciliation was elusive.

Hookes became a savvy media performer and an innovative coach but, sadly, was the first of the members of the Centenary Test team to die. He was indulging in the oldest of Australian rites, the post-match drink, when he was killed after being punched by a bouncer. Typically, he had been in the company of players from his current state, Victoria, and his former state after an ING game, doing what he had done since he first played state cricket 28 years before.

Hookes was only 48 years old and the outpouring of emotion that occurred after his death gives some insight into the way his role in the Centenary Test resonated with the Australian public. Hookes was player and person brim full of confidence. As Gary Cosier remembered, when Hookes walked into the dressing room full of stars for the Centenary Test, Hookes was no shrinking violet:

> Hookes was very edgy socially and on the field always pushing the envelope. It wasn't unusual for him to have a heated argument with one of the other players from time to time. He didn't overly speak his mind during the match. He had an interesting relationship with Kerry O'Keeffe who didn't always see eye to eye. There were times when neither would back off on their opinion and sometimes it got personal, they tolerated each other.

Hookes had everything Packer craved in a new cricket competition—he was a young, good looking, exciting cricketer to watch, photogenic, he had a cheeky charisma that made him stand out. While all this may have suited WSC, Hookes may well have been better off not signing.

When umpire Max O'Connell returned to work after the Centenary Test his Electricity Trust manager Ray Colyer contacted him to say he needed to see him. O'Connell thought he may have done something wrong. 'I opened the door to find eight Board executives sitting around a large table. I thought I was in trouble but all they wanted to know about was the game.'

While the financial remuneration was low—he was paid for $425 for the five days of the match plus $100 expenses to cover accommodation, travel and meals—O'Connell felt a little indulged having a room at the Hilton (normally he would find a billet in Melbourne).

O'Connell remembers the sound of the crowd at the MCG, amplified by the chanting of Lillee's name, making it sound more colosseum than cricket ground, and the way the crowd would bang their beer and soft drink cans on the metal fence.

He also remembers the theatrics of Lillee, who would pause after appealing for an lbw and also run by O'Connell and flick his umpire's hat off and smile. Max O'Connell umpired his final Test in 1980.

Kerry O'Keeffe's career was all but over after the 1977 Centenary Test. On the England tour that year he batted with greater application than most of his team-mates but made little impact with the ball. He joined WSC in 1977 and played mainly the up country matches and played little first-class cricket thereafter. In retirement he became an astute coach and commentator who developed an almost cult-like following with his unconventional way of broadcasting.

After the Centenary Test, Max Walker, with his unusual, wrong-footed action which prompted the nickname 'Tangles', managed just 14 test wickets at 39 on the 1977 tour of England. A useful batsman, his unbeaten 78 in the final test at the Oval exceeded expectations. This would be his last Test and, despite returning to first-class cricket after the reconciliation, Walker never managed to recreate the earlier form that would earn him another test cap. Walker's outgoing nature and ability to tell a yarn helped him to become an after-dinner speaker and a successful author of light-hearted books connected with sport. His participation in a television commercial added the phrase, 'Have a good weekend, Mr Walker' to everyday Australian speech. His naturalness on television led him to become a sports-show anchorman and television commentator.

Dennis Lillee didn't tour England in 1977 but held his form across two hectic and highly charged WSC summers and tours. The addition of World Series Cricket Supertest wickets (79 in 15 matches) proved what a force he still was.

Lillee kept playing first-class cricket until 1983–84 by modifying his action and shortening his run up. He developed an uncomplicated and economical approach to the wicket. His performance in capturing 39 wickets in six tests during Australia's 1981 tour of England, where he was often ill, proved again how good a bowler he was in adverse conditions.

His best test figures arrived in an amazing match against the West Indies in 1981. Lillee's figures were 4–10 at stumps, having dispatched Desmond Haynes, Faoud Bacchus, nightwatchman Colin Croft and, on the last ball of the day, he bowled Viv Richards. Lillee, who passed Gibbs' wicket-taking world record, ended up with 7–83 and ten wickets for the match as Australia recorded a famous win. Lillee now provides his bowling coaching expertise across the world. He made a brief comeback playing five games in 1987–88 for Tasmania where he took the wicket of Andrew Hilditch with his first ball.

Finishing with 355 wickets there was controversy when he kicked Pakistani Javed Miandad at the WACA in retaliation against Javed thrusting his bat handle into Lillee's ribs mid pitch. There was also Lillee's use of an aluminium bat in 1979–80 that proved an embarrassment to the game. His treatment of Kim Hughes as captain detracted from Lillee's overall performance as an Australia cricketer who gave his all to the game

Ray Bright, who was supposed to play a bit part as twelfth man in the Centenary Test, fielded for both of England's innings because of Rick McCosker's broken jaw. It didn't matter that Bright wasn't in the 11, he still views the match as one of his greatest thrills in cricket alongside the 1986 tied Test against India at Chepauk stadium in Madras. Bright took seven wickets in that match including five in the last innings as the Indians reached the total of 347. It was a match of many layers: Dean Jones' heroic 210; Boon and Border's centuries in stifling heat in Australia's first innings of 574; India's first innings response of 397, including a skipper's knock of 119 from Kapil Dev; and Greg Matthews' ten wickets for the match including the decisive final wicket of Maninder Singh lbw.

Bright remembers the tied Test, his last, (he was also the only remaining player from the 1977 Centenary Test sides playing Test cricket at the time) as 'full of emotion, heat and humidity'. Unlike the only other tied Test in history in 1960–61 between Australia and the West Indies, the players didn't have a great relationship with each other. Bright says he was lucky to have even played. The night before he had ordered a pizza and soon felt so sick he thought his world was going to end. Relieved when he found out Australia was batting first Bright spent the entire day (until he was called up to pad up as a nightwatchman) lying on the floor of Australia's spartan dressing room.

The Test was a highlight for Bright not only as it saw him bow out of Test cricket with personal success but also because of what he saw of then up-and-coming Dean Jones:

> *Jones' 210 was one of the best human endurances of all time, and he was still giving his all on the final day when he caught Gavaskar off a leading edge from my bowling on the last day where he had to dive full length.*

Ironically, only grainy highlights of the match remain and a well-made documentary by Mike Coward featuring the main contributors from the match.

Bright was one of only two who played in all the Australian Supertests in World Series Cricket. His Test career, though, finished with the modest figures of 53 wickets at 41.

THE ENGLAND PLAYERS

England's captain Tony Greig bowed out of test cricket in 1977 with scores against the Australians of 5, 91 76, 11, 0, 43, and 0. It was as if the pressure of the British cricket establishment and press, as well as being stripped of the English captaincy, had taken its toll.

Greig became an important negotiator, publicist and player for WSC. He settled in Sydney, and behind the microphone, to become an integral part of the Channel Nine commentary team. His provocative style, pre-match pitch reports and post-match interviews gained him huge publicity. He stayed in various commentary roles and was famously imitated by the Australia comedian Billy Birmingham in his Twelfth Man series. Throughout his life he was also be constantly reminded that he was struck for five fours in a row by David Hookes during the Centenary Test.

Greig died of a heart attack (having been suffering from lung cancer) on 29 December 2012 aged 66.

Bob Woolmer's test career was progressing well when he signed with Kerry Packer's World Series Cricket. In 1977 he scored hundreds in successive tests against Australia at Lord's and Old Trafford. But while Woolmer gained financially by joining WSC, he lost the momentum of his test career. As a batsman he was compared with Colin Cowdrey—he drove the ball fluently on the off side and worked the ball well off his legs. He finished though with a modest average of 33 from 19 tests. Woolmer was also a useful medium pacer and a competent close-in fielder. After the reconciliation Woolmer played just four more tests for England at home but failed to establish himself. He went on to coach Kent and Warwickshire and later South Africa and Pakistan. Match fixer, Hansie Cronje, was the captain during Woolmer's tenure as South Africa's coach. Woolmer died suddenly in Jamaica during the 2007 World Cup after Pakistan's elimination against Ireland.

Mike Brearley, it was said, rejected a vague offer to join Kerry Packer and recruit other members of the England team. If this is true it was one of the best decisions he ever made. When Tony Greig was stripped of the captaincy when news of the WSC signings leaked, Brearley took over, leading England to a 3–1 win. Although he failed to justify his place as a top England batsman, his clear thinking and calmness under pressure made him an excellent captain.

He led England to a 5–1 win against a weakened Australia in 1978–79 and in 1981 guided England from a 1–0 deficit after two tests to a 3–1 win, securing the Ashes. This was Brearley at his best; when he was at Headingley and Edgbaston he pressured the Australian batsmen with astute field placings and made the most of Willis and Botham as bowlers. Although Brearley had one of his best series as a batsman when England toured Australia in 1979–80, England lost the non-Ashes series 0–3. Brearley retired from first-class cricket in 1982 when he led Middlesex to its fourth championship under his stewardship. Brearley's scholarly mind led Rodney Hogg to remark that he had a 'degree in people'. He went on to work as a psychotherapist, freelance writer and lecturer. His book *The Art of Captaincy* is seen as one of the best of its kind.

Derek Randall was indeed England's hero of the Centenary Test. Despite this he experienced a modest series against Australia at home in 1977 followed by disappointing performances on the winter tour of Pakistan and New Zealand. In Sydney in 1978–79 Randall scored 150 in 589 minutes, which turned a delicately balanced series England's way. Randall was known for eccentricities that included talking to himself out loud and fidgeting about the crease when the bowler delivered. He had a poor tour of Australia in 1979–80 with scores of 0, 1, 0, and 25. Going in at number six in 1982 he hit hundreds for England against India at Lord's and as an opener against Pakistan at Edgbaston. On his fourth tour to Australia in 1982–83 he made 365 runs at 45 including 115 at Perth. Another century followed in a tussle with New Zealand. He finished with 47 tests at an average of 33.

For Keith Fletcher, with scores of 4 and 1, the Centenary Test remains best forgotten and for a period it ended his time as an England player. He was recalled to the England side as captain for the tour of 1981–82 where England lost the series 0–1. He did however lead England to success in the first ever Test played against Sri Lanka in February 1982 but after that was discarded. He was a canny captain of Essex during the 1980s, when he led them to several championship wins. He became England's coach in 1992 when he took over from Mickey Stewart but was sacked after England's defeat in Australia in 1996. As a Test batsman he finished with the respectable average of 39 from 59 Tests.

Dennis Amiss found success at the MCG when he scored 64 in England's second innings of the Centenary Test. However, he managed only 43 in two tests against Australia in 1977, ending his test career, that had seemed to have more highs and lows than most. Joining Kerry Packer, Amiss became one of the first to wear the motorcycle helmet while batting.

He could be considered unlucky not to have been selected again for England in the Post-Packer years, and joined the unofficial tour of South Africa in March 1982 where he headed the English batting averages. With his trademark abilities of a glorious cover drive and a strong flick off his pads, Amiss became the twenty-first cricketer to hit a hundred first-class hundreds in 1986 against Lancashire at Edgbaston. He served as Warwickshire's CEO for more than a decade and recruited Brian Lara as the county's overseas player. Amiss was later deputy chair of the England and Wales Cricket Board. Although Amiss often failed as a batsman against Australia, his average of 46 from 50 tests shows his class.

Despite signing up with WSC, England wicketkeeper Alan Knott played all five Tests of the 1977 Ashes scoring 135 at Trent Bridge in the Third Test. Reinstated after reconciliation, Knott's final test was against Australia in 1981. Seen as a 'gloveman apart', much of Knott's keeping was to the awkward bowling of Derek Underwood. Knott's 269 test victims and average of 32, with five centuries, saw him go down in history as one of England's best keepers. He retired from first-class cricket in 1985 to run his sports shop and gym. He was also a part-time coach, helping a succession of England wicketkeepers.

Knott's partner in crime, Derek Underwood, left the test arena after helping England win the 1977 Jubilee series against Australia but returned to play 12 more tests and to make two more tours, to Australia in 1979–80 and India in 1981–82. He joined the rebel tour to South Africa in 1982, which ended his test career on 297 wickets. He continued to play county cricket with Kent even scoring a first-class hundred against Sussex at the age of 39. In 2009 he served a one-year term as a president of the MCC.

Chris Old's time as a Test cricketer also ended when he joined the rebel tour of South Africa in 1982, having spent the 1981–82 winter playing for Northern Transvaal. He had moved from the status of genuinely quick to fast medium by the time he took 7–50, including four wickets in five balls, against Pakistan at Edgbaston in 1978. In 1981 he became captain of Yorkshire and played a valuable all-round role for England in exciting Test victories over Australia at Headingley and Edgbaston. He was often troubled by injury throughout his career and announced his retirement from first-class cricket after the 1985 season. Old was the only Englishman to play in both Centenary Tests (Dennis Lillee, Greg Chappell and Rod Marsh were the Australians who did so).

John Lever, who arrived on the test scene in spectacular fashion by taking 26 wickets at 14 on England's 1976–77 tour of India, would, in his 16 subsequent tests, take 47 wickets at a cost of 33. He was a hard worker on his five major tours between 1976 and 1982 but was also banned for three years after touring South Africa in 1982. He could swing the ball both ways in helpful conditions and was always accurate. In 1970 he helped Essex to a championship title by taking 106 wickets and continued his success passing 1500 first-class wickets in 1985. A year later he was recalled to the England line-up taking six wickets in England's 279 run loss to India at Leeds. He retired from first-class cricket at the end of the 1989 season and became a coach at an Essex school.

Lever told Cricinfo in 2015 of his memories of the England tour that included the Centenary Test:

> We wanted to go home but there was this centenary game tacked on to the end of it (subcontinent tour), which was pretty hard to get up for. Seeing all those players from times gone by, all getting pissed as farts, enjoying every dinner, didn't make it easy for us who were trying to get away from the dinners.

Bob Willis took 27 wickets at 19.77 against Australia in England in 1977 and then 20 wickets at 23.05 in Australia in 1978–79. He struggled against Australia in 1979–80 taking only three wickets at 74 but bounced back into the spotlight in 1981. It was at Headingley that Willis took 8–43 in Australia's second innings, bowling England to an amazing win against the odds. Australia were 1–56 chasing 130 to win when Willis, charging down the slope at the Kirkstall end, bowled fiercely with steepling bounce. Australia was bowled out for 111. Willis completed the series with 29 wickets. Appointed England captain in 1982, he started out by winning both series against India and Pakistan taking 25 wickets. He led England to Australia in 1982–83 where England lost the Ashes but Willis was again England's most successful bowler. In 1983 he became the fourth to take 300 wickets and ended his test career against the barnstorming 1984 West Indies side and later went on to become a professional television commentator.

Graham Barlow played the last of his three tests against Australia at Lord's in 1977 scoring one and five. Barlow failed to make much of an impact at Test level but, when at his best, his left-handed batting could be punishing. He was also highly effective fielder at cover and mid wicket and worked well in tandem with Derek Randall. He was an important member of the Middlesex sides that won championships five times between 1976 and 1985 but a serious back injury caused his retirement the following year. He later coached at provincial level.

CHAPTER

RICK MCCOSKER REMEMBERS

Rick McCosker would be forever haunted to some extent because of the broken jaw he received in the Centenary Test and the fact that, despite being a more than capable opening batsman for Australia, most would remember him for coming out to bat again in the second innings, all bandaged up.

McCosker says he would do it all again, even in the light of the death of Phil Hughes. 'I don't think differently now…you don't think about those things at the time because you are invincible until something like this (Phil Hughes' death) happens.'

After the Centenary Test McCosker copped some criticism that he had put Tony Greig and the English bowlers in a difficult position by going out to bat. But as McCosker says, this was a Test between Australia and England and he didn't expect to be looked after. He wanted to score runs and believes anyone else in the team would have done the same thing.

It was only afterwards that McCosker gave any thought to what would have happened had he been hit again, that 'he probably wouldn't be too good'. In some ways, for Rick McCosker the Centenary Test is a matter of regret. He fears he's been remembered for little else:

> People are put in boxes and that is the box they have put
> me in. There were other things I did in Test cricket that I
> thought were a hell of a lot better than that. After all I only

*scored 29 runs, out twice. That in itself is a pretty poor
effort compared to the other Tests I played in. Me batting
with an injury in the Centenary Test tends to overshadow
anything else I may have done.*

McCosker finds, 40 years later, he is always introduced at a speaking
event in the context of the Centenary Test: 'Being remembered for
something good is better than being remembered for some of the other
things players have done that haven't been that positive.'

After playing World Series Cricket McCosker made a brief return to
Test cricket in 1979–80 but his Test career ended when he was dropped
after the first Test against the West Indies in 1982. McCosker played only
25 Test matches over a five-year period (two of which were interrupted
by WSC). Over the years cricket fans appreciated his solid defence and
ability to score freely on the leg side. After ending his first-class career in
1983–84 he became an occasional cricket commentator before life took
him off in quite a different direction.

When he finished playing cricket McCosker was involved in and
then set up a building business. Post retirement he completed a three-
year Christian formation course and was asked to take on a position
of chaplain at the Port of Newcastle through the Catholic Diocese of
Maitland in Newcastle. There he works at an ecumenical mission centre
with a couple of Anglican priests and they provide practical and pastoral
care for all the seafarers that come into Newcastle port (the busiest coal
port in the world):

*We do whatever we can for the guys because they lead
a very tough and unrewarding life. I've always wanted
to do something worthwhile for somebody else and this
happened to come along at the right place and at the
right time.*

McCosker's faith put him at odds with the beer-swilling, sledging 'ugly

Australians' who smoked and drank to their heart's delight. McCosker, who didn't smoke and drank in moderation, was allowed to be whoever he wanted to be. 'It wasn't one in all in. There was a group of guys who smoked and drank more than others but there were people like me who didn't drink much.'

THE CENTENARY TEST IN THE CONTEXT OF CRICKET HISTORY

Without knowing it at the time, the 1977 Centenary Test proved to be a significant turning point in the history of cricket. The game was changing and would never return to its largely amateur status. As we now know, Kerry Packer and his acolytes used the Centenary Test to sign up the cream of Australian cricketing talent for World Series Cricket. When the news broke in May of 1977 the game was torn asunder as players, officials and spectators grappled with what the future might hold. As Packer battled the various cricket Boards through the courts, Australian cricket fans were divided, not knowing what the outcome of all the signings would be.

When it became clear two competing Australian competitions would come to be in the summer of 1977–78, cricket fans largely sided with the Australian Test players as they took on and defeated a full-strength Indian side in a thrilling series 3–2. For two long years Packer's WSC and the Australian Cricket Board waged a war that cost Packer six million dollars while the ACB lost more than $800,000 in lost revenues. Australia's establishment cricketers battled it out against full-strength international sides winning just one series out of the five they played. Packer's WSC, despite initially playing to minuscule crowds, through the vehicles of night and one-day cricket attracted broad interest and a more diverse demographic. When peace was brokered in May 1979 Kerry Packer had clearly won the war, buying out the exclusive television rights to Australian Test matches

For players, the win was more symbolic than financial. Australian Test cricketers' wages had doubled during WSC, with a larger match fee and more sizable bonuses. But the dramatic wages delivered to the WSC players during the Packer years were not maintained. In fact, it was not until a fully-fledged players' association was developed in 1997, and later the development of the Indian Premier League with the growth of Twenty-20 cricket, that players' incomes increased to the amounts we have today. But a shift had occurred in the way that players were perceived by administrators. No longer was it assumed that players would play for honour alone and it became clear there was a financial price for the Australian Cricket Board.

As McGilvray later lamented, 'the game is not the same', which echoed the view that the time of ACB rule without question had ended. Some might argue that the game had changed on the field as well, although essentially you still had to bowl a ball, hit a ball and field a ball. One obvious change was the increasing demand on players for an ever-crowded schedule. Such was the change that in the first season of the reconciliation Kim Hughes was not available for any games for his grade or state sides.

In 1981 Greg Chappell controversially asked his brother Trevor to bowl an underarm delivery to guarantee Australia won the second of a three-match series against New Zealand at the MCG. He later defended the move saying that the demanding pressure on the players as they criss-crossed the country playing a mixture of Test and one-day internationals had caused him to not be thinking straight.

The way the game was marketed had also altered. Cricketers became not just sportsmen but also celebrities. Cricketers were marketable as individuals. Playing schedules were changed to ensure that a one-day 'world series' of matches was played between Australia and two visiting nations each summer. Test matches and one-day games were interspersed with no real sense of logic in mind, merely the commercial imperative. One-day cricket at night became a feature of the Australian summer. With the increase in the number of one-day games came sharper fielding and better running between the wickets. A crammed schedule meant international players played less first-class cricket for their states and rarely, if ever, for their grade side. This removed what had previously been a passing on of a cricket culture and also deprived younger players of the chance to learn by competing against Test players at grade level.

Ironically, the value of the baggy green both by the players and financially continued to grow after the reconciliation. It was one element of the anti-establishment attitude of the Chappell-led era that faded, as the respect for the traditions of the game and its symbols strengthened.

Cricket as a game grew in popularity becoming more accessible to women and a younger demographic through the vehicle of one-day cricket. Cricket had become more entertaining and, as a result, was considered less stuffy and anachronistic by the mainstream audience.

Players also became more professional in their approach to training. The days of a few catches and a ten-minute bowling and batting session in the nets as a preparation for a Test match were over. The side to initially benefit the most was the West Indies, who brought together a perfect storm of wonderfully talented fast bowlers and aggressive yet controlled batsmen, brought to their peak with the fitness and physical requirements Packer demanded of his players during WSC. No longer would the West Indies be referred to with the derogatory description of Calypso cricketer, in reference to an ability to play exciting if not substantial cricket. Their cricket would now be played with ruthlessness.

Packer had changed the way we watched cricket. There were now multiple camera angles, constant replays, graphics to explain the game, commentary that was directed at newcomers to the game, pitch microphones, cricketers in coloured clothing facing a white ball at night and fielding restrictions to encouraged lofted strokes. Cricket had moved from the strictly sporting sphere to entertainment, lights and all.

It could be argued that what Packer began in 1977 with WSC and the introduction of day night and one-day cricket has led us to where we are now with the increasing amount of Twenty/20 cricket crammed into the season. The cricket authorities have long known what can bring money into the game and now it is up to them to ensure the game in its traditional form survives. Otherwise, we are in danger of losing the spectacle of classic contests such as the one provided by the players who took part in the 1977 Centenary Test.

Centenary Test Scorecard

Australia v England
Australia won by 45 runs
Test no. 800 | 1976–77 season
Played at Melbourne Cricket Ground
12, 13, 14, 16, 17 March 1977 (5-day match)

Australia 1st innings		R	M	B	4s	6s	SR
IC Davis	lbw b Lever	5	28	22	0	0	22.72
RB McCosker	b Willis	4	33	17	0	0	23.52
GJ Cosier	c Fletcher b Lever	10	19	10	2	0	100.00
GS Chappell*	b Underwood	40	234	139	0	0	28.77
DW Hookes	c Greig b Old	17	32	19	2	0	89.47
KD Walters	c Greig b Willis	4	14	8	0	0	50.00
RW Marsh†	c †Knott b Old	28	91	56	3	0	50.00
GJ Gilmour	c Greig b Old	4	24	20	0	0	20.00
KJ O'Keeffe	c Brearley b Underwood	0	2	2	0	0	0.00
DK Lillee	not out	10	59	53	1	0	18.86
MHN Walker	b Underwood	2	14	14	0	0	14.28
Extras	(b 4, lb 2, nb 8)	14					
Total	(all out; 43.6 overs)	138	(2.36 runs per 6 balls)				

Fall of wickets: 1–11 (Davis), 2–13 (McCosker), 3–23 (Cosier), 4–45 (Hookes), 5–51 (Walters), 6–102 (Marsh), 7–114 (Gilmour), 8–117 (O'Keeffe), 9–136 (Chappell), 10–138 (Walker)

Bowling	O	M	R	W	Econ	
JK Lever	12	1	36	2	2.25	
RGD Willis	8	0	33	2	3.09	(4nb)
CM Old	12	4	39	3	2.43	(6nb)
DL Underwood	11.6	2	16	3	1.02	

England 1st innings		R	M	B	4s	6s	SR
RA Woolmer	c Chappell b Lillee	9	43	30	1	0	30.00
JM Brearley	c Hookes b Lillee	12	64	40	1	0	30.00
DL Underwood	c Chappell b Walker	7	28	18	1	0	38.88
DW Randall	c †Marsh b Lillee	4	35	20	0	0	20.00
DL Amiss	c O'Keeffe b Walker	4	18	18	0	0	22.22
KWR Fletcher	c †Marsh b Walker	4	44	27	0	0	14.81
AW Greig*	b Walker	18	24	20	3	0	90.00
APE Knott†	lbw b Lillee	15	59	45	0	0	33.33
CM Old	c †Marsh b Lillee	3	27	17	0	0	17.64
JK Lever	c †Marsh b Lillee	11	39	25	2	0	44.00
RGD Willis	not out	1	20	17	0	0	5.88
Extras	(b 2, lb 2, w 1, nb 2)	7					
Total	(all out; 34.3 overs)	95	(2.07 runs per 6 balls)				

Fall of wickets: 1–19 (Woolmer), 2–30 (Brearley), 3–34 (Underwood), 4–40 (Amiss), 5–40 (Randall), 6–61 (Greig), 7–65 (Fletcher), 8–78 (Old), 9–86 (Knott), 10–95 (Lever)

Bowling	O	M	R	W	Econ	
DK Lillee	13.3	2	26	6	1.45	
MHN Walker	15	3	54	4	2.70	
KJ O'Keeffe	1	0	4	0	3.00	
GJ Gilmour	5	3	4	0	0.60	(2nb)

Australia 2nd innings		R	M	B	4s	6s	SR
IC Davis	c †Knott b Greig	68	238	153	6	0	44.44
KJ O'Keeffe	c Willis b Old	14	50	36	1	0	38.88
GS Chappell*	b Old	2	15	14	0	0	14.28
GJ Cosier	c †Knott b Lever	4	35	27	0	0	14.81
KD Walters	c †Knott b Greig	66	213	143	5	0	46.15
DW Hookes	c Fletcher b Underwood	56	122	69	9	0	81.15
RW Marsh†	not out	110	295	173	10	0	63.58
GJ Gilmour	b Lever	16	44	31	1	0	51.61
DK Lillee	c Amiss b Old	25	86	56	3	0	44.64
RB McCosker	c Greig b Old	25	85	68	3	0	36.76
MHN Walker	not out	8	27	24	0	0	33.33
Extras	(lb 10, nb 15)	25					
Total	(9 wickets dec; 96.6 overs)	419	(3.24 runs per 6 balls)				

Fall of wickets: 1–33 (O'Keeffe), 2–40 (Chappell), 3–53 (Cosier), 4–132 (Davis), 5–187 (Walters), 6–244 (Hookes), 7–277 (Gilmour), 8–353 (Lillee), 9–407 (McCosker)

Bowling	O	M	R	W	Econ	
JK Lever	21	1	95	2	3.39	
RGD Willis	22	0	91	0	3.10	(8nb)
CM Old	27.6	2	104	4	2.81	(9nb)
AW Greig	14	3	66	2	3.53	(3nb)
DL Underwood	12	2	38	1	2.37	

England 2nd innings (target: 463 runs)		R	M	B	4s	6s	SR
RA Woolmer	lbw b Walker	12	47	36	1	0	33.33
JM Brearley	lbw b Lillee	43	170	142	2	0	30.28
DW Randall	c Cosier b O'Keeffe	174	446	353	21	0	49.29
DL Amiss	b Chappell	64	227	185	3	0	34.59
KWR Fletcher	c †Marsh b Lillee	1	12	8	0	0	12.50
AW Greig*	c Cosier b O'Keeffe	41	100	82	7	0	50.00
APE Knott†	lbw b Lillee	42	81	51	5	0	82.35
CM Old	c Chappell b Lillee	2	5	4	0	0	50.00
JK Lever	lbw b O'Keeffe	4	15	25	0	0	16.00
DL Underwood	b Lillee	7	21	19	0	0	36.84
RGD Willis	not out	5	10	5	1	0	100.00
Extras	(b 8, lb 4, w 3, nb 7)	22					
Total	(all out; 112.4 overs)	417	(2.78 runs per 6 balls)				

Fall of wickets: 1–28 (Woolmer), 2–113 (Brearley), 3–279 (Amiss), 4–290 (Fletcher), 5–346 (Randall), 6–369 (Greig), 7–380 (Old), 8–385 (Lever), 9–410 (Underwood), 10–417 (Knott)

Bowling	O	M	R	W	Econ	
DK Lillee	34.4	7	139	5	3.02	(1nb)
MHN Walker	22	4	83	1	2.82	
GJ Gilmour	4	0	29	0	5.43	(6nb)
GS Chappell	16	7	29	1	1.35	
KJ O'Keeffe	33	6	108	3	2.45	(1nb)
KD Walters	3	2	7	0	1.75	(2nb)

Balls per over 8

Toss England, who chose to field

Result Australia won the 1976–77 Centenary Test

Test debut DW Hookes (Australia)

Player of the match DW Randall (England)

Umpires TF Brooks and MG O'Connell

Close of play

- **Sat. 12 March,** day 1—England 1st innings 29–1 (JM Brearley 12*, DL Underwood 5*)
- **Sun. 13 March,** day 2—Australia 2nd innings 104–3 (IC Davis 45*, KD Walters 32*)
- **Mon. 14 March,** day 3—Australia 2nd innings 387–8 (RW Marsh 95*, RB McCosker 17*)
- **Tue. 15 March**—rest day
- **Wed. 16 March,** day 4—England 2nd innings 191–2 (DW Randall 87*, DL Amiss 34*)
- **Thu. 17 March,** day 5—England 2nd innings 417 (112.4 ov). End of match.

BIBLIOGRAPHY

Annuals

Baggy Green, Whimpress, Bernard 1997–2004; *Wisden Cricketers' Almanack* 1976, 1977, 1978

Newspapers and Magazines

1977 Centenary Test Program: Official Souvenir Publication of the Australian Cricket Board; ABC Cricket Book 1975–1980; Australian Cricket 1975–1980; Cricketer (Australia 1975–1980); Cricketer (UK); The Advertiser; The Age; The Australian; The Guardian; The Sydney Morning Herald; Time Magazine, March 1977; *World of Cricket 1977–80*

Interviews

Dennis Amiss, Mike Brearley, Ray Bright, Greg Chappell, Gary Cosier, Ian Davis Rick McCosker Peter Ovenden Max O'Connell Alan Shiell, Doug Walters, Derek Underwood,

DVDs and CDs

ABC audio *AM* program, March 1977

BBC Sport Audio, July 2013

Cricket in the 70's—The Chappell Era, ABC TV, 2002.

Frank Crook Interviews, ABC Grandstand 1989

John Arlott's Cricketing Wides, Byes and Slips!, BBC audio May, 2009

Spirit of the Ashes: The Mystique, The Decisive Matches, And The Men Who Won Them, Jack Egan, Wilkinson Publishing Pty Ltd, 2006

Books

Amiss, Dennis. *In Search of Runs: an autobiography (with Michael Carey),* Stanley Paul and Co Ltd, London, 1976.

Bateman, Anthony and Hill Jeffery (editors). *The Cambridge Companion to Cricket,* Cambridge University Press, 2011.

Barker, Ralph. *Innings of a Lifetime,* Collins, London, 1982.

Barry, Paul. *The Rise and Rise of Kerry Packer Uncut,* Bantam, Sydney, 2007.

Batchelder, Alf; Rusden, Ann; Webster, Ray. *The Centenary Test, Melbourne Cricket Ground March 1977,* MCC Library, Melbourne Cricket Club, East Melbourne, 2002.

Beecher, Eric. *The Cricket Revolution: The Inside Story of the Great Cricket Crisis of 1977–78,* Newspress, Melbourne, 1978.

Brayshaw, Ian. *The Miracle Match: Chappell, Lillee, Richards and the most electric moment in Australian cricket history*, Hardie Grant, Melbourne, 2014.

Brearley, Mike and Doust, Dudley. *The Return of the Ashes,* Pelham Books, London, 1977.

Cartledge, Eliot *Footy's Glory Days: The Greatest Era of the Greatest Game* Hardie Grant, Melbourne, 2013.

Cashman, Richard; Franks, Warwick; Maxwell, Jim; Stoddart, Brian; Weaver, Amanda; Webster, Ray (ed). *The Oxford Companion to Australian Cricket,* Oxford University Press, Sydney, 1996.

Chappell, Greg and Frith, David. *The Ashes '77,* Angus and Robertson, London, 1977.

Chappell, Greg, *The 100th Summer,* Gary Sparke and Associates, Melbourne, 1977.

Chappell, Greg. *Fierce Focus,* Hardie Grant, Melbourne, 2011.

Coward, Mike. *The Chappell Years, Cricket in the '70s,* ABC Books, Sydney, 2002.

Davis, Charles (compiler). *Test Cricket in Australia, 1877–2002: The Test Match Archive,* Charles Davis, Melbourne, 2002.

Davis, Ian. *More than Cricket: His Remarkable Story,* Brian Wood, 2004.

Egan, Jack. *Spirit of the Ashes: The mystique. The decisive matches. And the men who won them,* Wilkinson Publishing Pty Ltd, Melbourne, 2006.

Fletcher, Keith. *Captain's Innings: an autobiography,* Stanley Paul and Co Ltd, London, 1983.

Forsyth, Chris. *The Great Cricket Hijack,* Widescope, Melbourne, 1978.

Foster, David and Arnold, Peter. *100 Years of Test Cricket, England v Australia,* Hamlyn Publishing Group Ltd, 1984.

Fraser, Malcolm, and Simons, Margaret. *Malcolm Fraser: The Political*

Memoirs, Random House, Sydney, 2010

Fraser-Simpson, Guy. *Cricket at the Crossroads: Class, colour and controversy from 1967 to 1977,* Eliot and Thomson, London, 2011.

Frindall, Bill (ed). *The Wisden Book of Test Cricket 1877–1977: Volume 1,* Headline Publishing, London, 1995.

Frindall, Bill (ed). *The Wisden Book of Test Cricket 1997–1994: Volume 2,* Headline Publishing, London, 1995.

Frindall, Bill. *Frindall's Scorebook Jubilee Edition,* Lonsdale Press, London, 1977.

Gibbs, Barry. *My Cricket Journey*, Wakefield Press, Adelaide, 2001.

Greig, Joyce and Greig, Mark. *Tony Greig: Love, War and Cricket, a Family Memoir,* Pan Macmillan Australia Pty Ltd, Sydney, 2013.

Greig, Tony. *My Story,* Stanley Paul, London, 1980.

Haigh, Gideon. *Uncertain Corridors, Writings on Modern Cricket,* Penguin, Melbourne 2013.

Haigh, Gideon. *The Cricket War: The Inside Story of Kerry Packer's World Series Cricket*, Melbourne University Press, Melbourne, 2007.

Haigh, Gideon and Frith, David. *Inside Story: Unlocking Australian Cricket Archives,* New Custom Publishing, Melbourne, 2007.

Holmes, Bob and Marks, Vic (ed). *Fifty Cricket Stars Describe My Greatest Game,* Mainstream Publishing Company (Edinburgh) Ltd, 1995.

Hookes, David and Shiell, Alan. *Hookesy*, ABC Books, Sydney, 1993.

Juddery, Mark. *1975 Australia's Greatest Year,* John Wiley and Sons, Sydney, 2005.

Knott, Alan. *It's Knott Cricket*, Macmillan, London, 1985.

Lawry, Bill and Davis Ken. *Bill Lawry's Greatest Moments of Cricket*, Pan Macmillan Australia Pty Limited, Sydney.

Lazenby, John. *The Strangers Who Came Home: The First Australian Cricket Tour of England,* John Wisden and Co Ltd (an imprint of Bloomsbury Publishing Plc), London, 2015.

Lillee, Dennis. *Lillee: An Autobiography,* Hodder, Sydney, 2003.

McFarline, Peter. *A Game Divided,* Marlin Books, Melbourne, 1978.

Marchant, John. *The Greatest Test Match,* Faber and Gwyer, London, 1926.

Marsh, Rod. *Gloves, Sweat and Tears: The Final Shout,* Penguin, Sydney, 1984.

Martin-Jenkins, Christopher. *The Jubilee Tests,* MacDonald and Jane's, London, 1979.

Martin-Jenkins, Christopher. *World Cricketers: A Biographical Dictionary,* Oxford University Press, Oxford, 1996.

McGilvray, Alan. *The Game is Not the Same,* ABC Books, Sydney, 1985.

McGilvray, Alan & Tasker, Norm. *Alan McGilvray's Backpage of Cricket: 60 Golden Seasons,* Lester–Townsend Publishing Pty Ltd, Sydney, 1989.

Nicholls, Barry. *The Establishment Boys, The Other Side of Kerry Packer's Cricket Revolution,* New Holland Publishers, Sydney, 2015.

Nicholls, Barry. *You Only Get One Innings: Family, Mates and the Wisdom of Cricket,* Harper Collins, Sydney 2013.

Perry, Roland. *The Ashes: a Celebration,* Random House Australia, 2006.

Piesse, Ken and Davis, Charles. *Encyclopaedia of Australian Cricket Players,* New Holland Publishers, Sydney, 2012.

Randall, Derek. *The Sun Has Got His Hat On,* Willow Books, London, 1984.

Ryan, Christian. *Golden Boy: Kim Hughes and the Bad Old Days of Australian Cricket,* Hardie Grant, Melbourne, 2011.

Ryan, Christian (ed). *Australia: Story of a Cricket Country,* Hardie Grant, Melbourne 2012.

Tossell, David. *Tony Greig: A Reappraisal of English Cricket's Most Controversial Captain,* Pitch Publishing, Brighton, 2011.

Tyson, Frank. *The Centenary Test,* ACB Publications Sub-Committee, RJ Parish, RC Steele, LV Maddocks, Melbourne, 1977.

Various, *Remembering Hookesy,* Swan Sport, Queensland, 2004.

Walters, Doug. *The Doug Walters Story,* Rigby, Sydney, 1981.

Webster Ray (ed). *First-class Cricket in Australia Vol 2 1945–46 to 1976–77,* Ray Webster, Glen Waverly, 1997.

ACKNOWLEDGEMENTS

Forty years have passed since the Centenary Test that so enthralled the nation. It was a match I had closely followed as a cricket-mad 14-year-old and later wondered what made this contest as enduring as it has become. This book is an attempt to find out. It is also a look at a critical junction in the game's history when it was about to be torn apart by Kerry Packer's World Series Cricket. Unbeknown to the Australian cricket administrators, Aussie players were being signed by Packer and his associates throughout the celebration that was the Centenary Test!

My attempt here is to lead the reader back to the year of 1977, looking at events from not only cricketing perspective but also a social and to some extent political perspective.

It could not have been achieved without the generosity of former players Greg Chappell, Gary Cosier, Ian Davis, Rick McCosker, Ray Bright, Doug Walters, Mike Brearley, Derek Underwood and Dennis Amiss who kindly gave me their time as did former umpire Max O'Connell and journalists Alan Shiell and Peter Ovenden.

Three resources in particular were crucial to me being able to recreate the events of March 1977. Frank Tyson's contemporary account, *The Centenary Test,* the Melbourne Cricket Club Library's 2002 book *The Centenary Test, Melbourne Cricket Ground, March 1977* and the ABC DVD *Cricket in the 70s*, which included highlights of the match and interviews with former and present players.

Many thanks to New Holland Publishing, in particular to Alan Whiticker and Liz Hardy for their encouragement and patience and attention to detail. Ken Piesse has also been a great support and staff at the MCC library provided me with an MCC newsletter that contained some invaluable information. Sue Mercer trawled the Perth Library for contemporary accounts of the match and I thank her for that.

Finally, a special thank you to Ann, who not for the first time provided wonderful support and must have at times wondered when the Centenary Test of 1977 would finally be over.

ABOUT THE AUTHOR

Barry Nicholls is a broadcaster and journalist who presents a three-hour daily drive program on ABC. He also hosts a fortnightly half-hour podcast on sports writing for ABC *Grandstand*.

Barry has contributed articles for Fairfax and News Limited as well as publications including *Wisden Cricketers' Almanack*, *Inside Edge*, *Baggy Green*, *Cricket Lore* and *The Allrounder*.

He has written six well received books about sport which include *You Only Get One Innings: Family, Mates and the Wisdom of Cricket*, *For Those Who Wait —the Barry Jarman Story* and *The Establishment Boys: The Other Side of Kerry Packer's Cricket Revolution*.

First published in 2016 by New Holland Publishers Pty Ltd
London • Sydney • Auckland

The Chandlery Unit 704 50 Westminster Bridge Road London SE1 7QY United Kingdom
1/66 Gibbes Street Chatswood NSW 2067 Australia
5/39 Woodside Ave Northcote, Auckland 0627 New Zealand

www.newhollandpublishers.com

A record of this book is held at the British Library and the National Library of Australia.

ISBN 9781742577753

Managing Director: Fiona Schultz
Publisher: Alan Whiticker
Project Editor: Liz Hardy
Designer: Andrew Quinlan
Cover Design: Thomas Partridge
Production Director: James Mills-Hicks
Printer: Toppan Leefung Printing Ltd
10 9 8 7 6 5 4 3 2 1

Keep up with New Holland Publishers on Facebook
www.facebook.com/NewHollandPublishers